Words for Our Time

THE SPIRITUAL WORDS OF
MATTHEW THE POOR

CONCILIAR PRESS ✝ CHESTERTON, INDIANA

Words for Our Time
The Spiritual Words of Matthew the Poor

English translation copyright © 2012 by James Helmy

Published by:
    Ancient Faith Publishing
    (formerly known as Conciliar Press)
    A division of Ancient Faith Ministries
    P.O. Box 748
    Chesterton, IN 46304

Printed in the United States of America

ISBN 10: 1-936270-45-5
ISBN 13: 978-1-936270-45-3

20 19 18 17 16 15 14   10 9 8 7 6 5 4 3 2

For Marianne
—J.H.

Contents

An Introduction to
Father Matthew the Poor

IT IS NOT AN EASY TASK to acquaint the reader with the
extraordinarily wide spectrum of Matthew the Poor's work and
labor, as well as his influence on the church of Egypt and on the faith
worldwide. Those who had known the man intimately—clergy, laity,
politicians, philosophers, and unbelievers—strain to find words to
express their gratitude, their affection, and their boundless admiration
for a saint who forever changed their lives by his example, and who
will doubtless be recognized in later centuries as one of the giants
of the Alexandrian Church.

His life and works are admittedly unlike anything the Coptic
Church has produced for centuries; an impartial judgment will have
to concede that, to find a father of the Egyptian desert comparable
to Matthew the Poor's stature, one would have to go back to the days
of Athanasius, Cyril, and Antony the Great. His spiritual influence,
directly or indirectly, has permeated virtually every domain of Coptic
life in the twentieth century; there was scarcely a man of intellect or

prayer in the whole country in his day who could claim to have been untouched by his work. And this man, who took such great pains (sometimes literally) to flee publicity and position in the Church, was appointed by divine providence to serve as the chief reviver and patron of Coptic monasticism and spirituality for the modern era.

Mere uninhibited adulation, however, will not do justice to Fr. Matthew the Poor, or Abouna Matta el-Meskeen, as he is affectionately known in Egypt. In order to understand his significance, one must first of all personally read the works that have come from his pen and been made available in English, then move on to his detailed biography, which is pending translation and publication. To highlight the main points of that blessed and turbulent life is the chief aim of this introduction.

The English reader may be considered to be in a more comfortable position than the Arabic reader, because Abba Matta's works in Arabic are so extensive in number, so prodigious in bulk, and so multifarious in subject matter that it is impossible to cover them all. The major works include his seminal *Orthodox Prayer Life*, along with *The Life of Christ*; *The Life and Works of St. Paul*; *St. Athanasius the Apostolic*; *The Eucharist*; *Coptic Monasticism*; *The Psalms, Prophets and Prophecy*; and *The Titles of Christ*, in addition to lengthy commentaries on nearly the entire New Testament, as well as a host of smaller works on almost every spiritual subject under the sun.

FR. MATTHEW'S EARLY LIFE

Youssef Iskander, our subject's premonastic name, was born in upper Egypt at the close of the First World War, and already seemed to be marked out by divine providence for a life of spiritual vigor and abundance. His family was poor in belongings but rich in faith; his mother was a saintly woman who taught him to pray, and he recollects how he would stand to pray as a child whenever family troubles arose, filled with an acute awareness of a heavenly presence. His early youth was a time of rapid spiritual growth, though perhaps with only an incidental relationship with the official church. He still loved the world, as he says, and was particularly fond of walking along the Nile and spending time in beautiful gardens, wrapped in meditation. He enjoyed social events, music, fine clothing, and oil painting; in later years, the monks of one monastery entered his cell and found a sumptuous painting of the Roman saints Maximus and Dometius.

Youssef was of a congenial nature, according to the testimonies of his friends, and his amiable sociability won him a vast body of friends and acquaintances. He was remarked during his university years as a youth of uncommon decency and prudence, and he became a sort of father confessor to many of his peers, who approached him for counsel on personal issues. He dedicated his entire education to God's pleasure, and it was not unusual for him to interrupt his studies twenty to thirty times in an evening in response to an urge to rise and pray.

In 1943 he entered upon his professional career of pharmacist with the same tireless industry that marked his educational years. The poor and destitute flocked to him as the only pharmacist willing to drop his fees, at times even to nothing, to make accessible the medicines needed to ameliorate their ailing health. Divine favor granted him prosperity, as he eventually became the owner of two thriving pharmacies, two villas, and two automobiles—and this in the scanty days of the post-WWII era.

AN UNEXPECTED CHOICE

But the "spiritual pressure" and "awareness of eternal life," as he called them, began to rapidly increase in his heart, and he grew acutely dissatisfied with the status quo of life in the world. He desired only complete and unfettered devotion to God; and as far as he could see, monasticism was the only way to achieve it. The Egyptian desert of those days was a virtual wasteland, and the monasteries generally sat listlessly in a deplorable state of disrepair and neglect. They were daily susceptible to attack by Arab bandits; they lacked essential food and supplies; hardly any roads were present to provide safe transportation to them; and most of them were occupied by only five to ten monks at most, all uneducated.

The idea of a young, prosperous, and educated citizen of Alexandria abandoning everything to seek shelter in a monastery of that period was preposterous. When he revealed his secret wish to the metropolitan, the aged hierarch asked if he had not quite heard him right. When he announced his decision to his close friends, they made the inconsiderate suggestion that perhaps he had gone out of his mind. When the servants of his church discovered his plan, they derisively asked whether there was any useful occupation to be found in a monastery other than cooking. His acquaintances went so far as to form a coalition of forty persons to attempt to dissuade him from his path, but they could succeed only in provoking a temporary hesitation in his heart (by his own confession). If Abraham of old could go out by God's call, not knowing whither he went, Youssef said to himself, then so could he.

He thereupon took the critical step of transforming idea into action, sold every worldly possession for which he had worked so hard, gave all the proceeds to the poor save the fee for a one-way train ticket to the desert, and made his famous exodus from the world. Youssef had never before seen a monastery or even discoursed with a monk, but he knew what he wanted: the poorest and remotest monastic community in Egypt. He wanted to be seen by no one and known by no one, in order to offer himself entirely as a gift to God. Learning of an impoverished Deir Enba Samuel, the Monastery of St. Samuel the Confessor, he made the ten-hour camel ride required to reach the deserted spot. The five frail and elderly monks living there, who were unaccustomed to receiving any visitors, celebrated his arrival by ringing the church bells—an act normally reserved only for major feast days—which was a cordial sign of honor that brought tears to Youssef's eyes.

A ZEALOUS MONK

In Deir Enba Samuel, Abba Matta began cultivating an intense spirit of devotion to God and the Scriptures. His passion for praises led him to extended bouts of individual praising until he frequently exhausted every hymn and psalmody available in the books. He would read between thirty and fifty chapters of the Bible daily, using the dimmest oil lamp to last the entire night. He executed faithfully a regimen of 350 prostrations every night as prescribed by his spiritual director, Abouna Mina the Solitary (in later years Pope Kyrillos VI). His feats of spiritual activity were colossal; and they were carried out with such sheer intensity, and on such a sparse diet, that his knees would frequently give out at the end of the day.

He also nurtured the spirit of self-sacrifice, accepting the most menial tasks of which the older monks were incapable by reason of their infirmities. He took to washing their feet, and he personally cleansed the monastery's septic tank daily. The area was, in addition, extremely wild, and Youssef frequently found unwelcome visitors in his cell in the form of deadly serpents and scorpions. The extreme conditions and lack of proper nutrition under which Youssef labored subjected him to frequent illnesses; and so, in consideration of his well-being, his spiritual director ordered him to leave the forlorn wilderness for the more livable and renowned Deir el-Suryan in the desert of Scete.

Abba Matta settled into his new abode, and in a short time the abbot of the monastery, the celebrated Bishop Theophilus, developed a strong affection for the new monk. He expressed his desire to ordain Abba Matta a priest, but the young monk responded with adamant refusal. The abbot remonstrated repeatedly with Abba Matta to accept the honor, but he replied that he desired neither privilege nor position from the church, only a life of strict monasticism.

The exchange went on for some time until one evening during vespers, when the bishop requested a word with the young monk. The monk approached in obedience, then the bishop suddenly slapped his hand on his head and declared, "Abba Matta, I ordain you priest in the Monastery of el-Suryan!" Shocked and dismayed, Abba Matta fled to his cell and shut the door behind him. The bishop rushed to the cell with an entourage of monks, performed a prostration before the closed door, and pleaded with Abba Matta to accept the improvised ordination. He shouted back that he would not. The venerable bishop responded by shutting himself up in his own cell and refusing to eat or drink until Abba Matta would accept priesthood. Being informed that the bishop had thus humbly deprived himself for three days, Abba Matta had no choice but to comply with the bishop's will. It would later prove to be God's will as well.

Abba Matta, now Father Matta el-Meskeen, found his hunger for complete solitude fulfilled in a cell located forty minutes away from the monastery by foot. His spirit reveled in the quiet retreat afforded him by the stark desolation of the wilderness, and he spent the majority of his time in prayer, hymnology, and Bible reading. He returned to the monastery only once every forty days for celebration of the holy liturgy. During this period he completed his celebrated masterpiece, *Orthodox Prayer Life*, a compendium of patristic and mystical essays on the means, obstacles, and joys of prayer. The book—the first of its kind in Egypt to delve so deeply into mystical spirituality from a patristic standpoint—circulated quickly throughout Egypt and became an immediate sensation.

CALLED BACK TO THE WORLD

A copy of this book made its way all the way to the patriarch, Pope Yousab, who was so impressed by its content that he appointed Abba Matta to the then-vacant post of patriarchal deputy in Alexandria. The Coptic Pope is by virtue of title and history Bishop of Alexandria, but for practical purposes resides in Cairo, the modern administrative center of the country. His corporeal absence from Alexandria is compensated for by the installment of a deputy or representative in his place, thus ensuring that the episcopal duties required for the immense city are performed, without violating the Nicene canon that prohibits two bishops from occupying the same diocese. Thus at the age of thirty-five, the young Abba Matta took on the responsibilities that historically devolved upon the Coptic patriarch.

He was welcomed, of course, with all the festivity and fanfare that normally accompany the arrival of a new bishop to an eastern diocese. Despite a mere fourteen-month tenure, Abba Matta implemented a stunning array of reforms and innovations that have shaped the Alexandrian church till the present day. He personally mentored one of Egypt's brightest stars in the twentieth century, Fr. Bishoy Kamel; and together they purchased land for what would become Alexandria's most fertile church in piety and publications, St. George's Church in Sporting. He also revived the defunct theological school of Alexandria, which had lain dormant since the sixth century, and instituted reforms that rehabilitated the lives of married couples and priests.

Sadly, however, this was the stage in which began all of Abba Matta's troubles. A clandestine faction had subsisted below the surface of the church which, like Diotrephes, loved the preeminence, as well as power, and sought to enlist Abba Matta and his popularity as agents in the pursuit of their aims. He naturally loathed all such ambition for power; and when they approached him in his office with their tantalizing offer, he immediately dismissed them from the room. The offense could not be forgiven. Joining forces with a set of disgruntled Alexandrian priests who resented his reforming spirit, these newly formed antagonists rapidly secured a patriarchal order for his removal from the city. His reputation and inimitable spirituality were now a threat to their designs; and the devout soul suddenly found himself the object of a merciless campaign of calumny and maltreatment which was to last almost till his dying day.

RETURN TO THE MONASTERY

Abba Matta returned to Deir el-Suryan to the great joy of its admiring abbot, Bishop Theophilus. He immediately appointed Abba Matta to the role of spiritual director of all the monks, a duty normally reserved for the bishop, despite Matta's many protests. The monastery soon underwent a bright flowering. As director, he oversaw the cleanup and renovation of the entire premises, which had lain in shambles. The monks were placed under a new spiritual rule; the library was transformed; and the study of hymnody was revived by the invitation of Egypt's most famous cantor, Mikhail the Great. It was a time of monastic renaissance. Egypt's young men began flocking to Deir el-Suryan to join in what was deemed to be a historic return to the roots of Coptic monasticism.

But Abba Matta's sincere efforts ultimately did not play in his favor. Jealousy and spite, those chronic maladies of man, swelled the breasts of the older monks of the monastery, as well as of the other three monasteries in Scete, which together had barely five monks added to their numbers during the same period. A covert conspiracy was once again organized against Abba Matta, and a general rumor was diffused which alleged that he and his disciples were planning to stage a coup of the monastery. Alarmed and dismayed, Abba Matta immediately renounced all his leadership rights in the monastery and shut himself up in a cell for seventy continuous days.

A SMALL BAND OF FOLLOWERS

Once the pressure against him reached a critical level, he decided it best to abandon the monastery altogether. He revealed his decision to his distraught disciples, strictly forbade anyone from following after him, and quietly left in the middle of the night. He found temporary refuge in the House of Dedication in Cairo, a religious establishment he had personally founded for the support of those who wished to lead celibate lives for the service of the church. But he was soon surprised by the appearance of a band of twelve of his most loyal disciples from Deir el-Suryan, who had traced his footsteps without his knowledge. They had sworn not to live anywhere again away from his presence. The leader of the little group was Abba Antonios el-Suryani, who in later times would be elevated to the patriarchal chair.

The story of Abba Matta and his small band of followers becomes extremely convoluted and confusing for the next few years. Continually stalked and besieged by their untiring adversaries, they were rudely shoved from place to place, and prevented by a series of executive orders from ever feeling secure or settled anywhere. It now dawned on Abba Matta that in order to live in peace and to achieve the simple life of solitude he had always desired, the group needed to relocate to the most remote and inaccessible desert possible that would harbor human life. He enlisted the aid of a renowned geologist and discovered that their destination was Wadi el-Rayan—a barren and austere valley located in the uninhabited wastelands of upper Egypt. Here began ten of the toughest years of Abba Matta's life.

Soon after the band arrived at their new home, they were hailed by a nomadic Arab who by chance, or rather by providence, happened to be in the vicinity. After failing to convince them that no human being could ever survive in such a hostile place, the stranger led them to a large cave in the mountain that would serve as their chief abode. After months of hard labor, they managed to dig individual cells out of the mountainside for the personal residence of each monk. Only the most intimate and trusted friends in Egypt now knew where the monks lived, and they would pay them a visit every several months with gifts of food and medicine. In better times, their daily fare would consist of two small loaves, a spoonful of honey, seven olives, and a piece of cheese the size of a matchbox. In scarcer times, their diet became extremely tenuous, until God would heed their cries for help and send an apostle of life to provide the bare essentials. They grew a small garden of vegetables that provided the basic nutrients to stave off disease, and they dug a well for their water supply.

Their daily existence was beset by a strange assortment of hazards, including sandstorms, massive wolves and serpents, and the threat of marauding Arabs bearing rifles. To add to their trials, they learned that an ambiguous source in the hierarchy had rented a slot in the advertising section of Egypt's national paper, *Al-Ahram*, to post an announcement stating that Abba Matta was officially stripped of his priesthood, his monks were stripped of their monastic rank, and the group was formally unrecognized and unsupported by the church. They were now officially cut off from the succor of Christ's Body; they were like so many orphans disowned and cast away.

The great severity of the injustice served to Abba Matta, along with the external hardships, were enough to stretch an average man's nerves to bursting; but the suffering saint exhibited an incredible resilience and positivity in what he often referred to as the shadow of death. "The Lord has honored me exceedingly," he once told his monks, "in allowing me to undergo unjust hardships and persecutions dealt by Satan and by man. . . . I have reached the point of suffocation and death, but I have also reached the state of true thanksgiving and full contentment." Regarding the day he was informed of the newspaper statement, he says, "It was one of the best days of my life, because I spent the entire day [praying] on the top of the mountain; and I sold myself to Christ."

The little band went on with their daily lives in Wadi el-Rayan, toiling all day alongside their spiritual father as they listened to the spiritual words he spoke to them. One day in 1969 their destiny took a dramatic turn for the better, when Abba Matta was obligated to travel to Cairo for medical treatment. He was approached by the patriarch's secretary and informed that Pope Kyrillos had been lately experiencing a restless anxiety on account of their plight. The saintly prelate would often wake suddenly in the middle of the night, in a state of alarm and grief, and call for his secretary to ask whether Abba Matta and his disciples were well.

Abba Matta went to meet the Coptic Pope, and the latter, in a gesture of humility and compunction, brought the great weight of his patriarchal authority to the floor, and made a prostration before the lowly monk. The pope begged forgiveness from Abba Matta for the mistreatment he had endured at the hands of the church. He ordered his followers to leave the dry valley they had inhabited for ten years and move to Deir Abu Makar, the Monastery of St. Macarius. God had not forsaken his orphans.

A NEW MONASTIC HOME

Abba Matta and his disciples arrived at the site to find an establishment on the verge of collapse. The buildings were dilapidated, the facilities were old and unusable, and the crumbling walls were hedged in by even larger walls of sand that pressed dangerously against them. The ancient monastery, due to its dreadful condition and long history of inaction, rarely received visitors, and the six elderly monks who inhabited the site had despaired of ever seeing a new candidate for monasticism enter their gate. Seeing now a band of twelve younger monks coming to join them, the monastery's abbot ordered the head cantor to receive them with hymns of joy. They took Abba Matta's group through the monastery grounds in a procession of celebration; voices were uplifted, spirits were high, and Abba Matta remarked that he felt as though St. Macarius himself shouted from the grave.

The story of the complete rebuilding of the Monastery of St. Macarius requires a book, or at least a separate essay, in itself. It is a marvelous story full of vision, faith, perseverance, labor, and an endless series of miracles. Indeed, the monastery as it now appears before the viewer's eye is a work of wonder. How a handful of penniless monks could transform a deteriorated compound into a lively and flourishing center of spirituality—an enterprise that required over one hundred million Egyptian pounds—is nearly incomprehensible.

When Abba Matta first presented to his fellow monks a set of his conceptual drawings for the reconstruction of the monastery, they were simply incredulous and told him the type of monastery he envisaged could be built only in one's dreams. But as his biographer later remarked, Abba Matta's faith could see things that no one else could see. His philosophy of work is best expressed in his own words: "What is the importance of a given work? For even if it fails, the important thing is that you succeed. However, I am certain that if you are faithful, joyful, and zealous—even if human weakness causes you to make mistakes—the work will succeed!"

ABBA MATTA'S "WORDS"

Abba Matta never gave what we would properly call a "sermon." This was a point he insisted on with the utmost persistence. "I am not sermonizing you, brethren," he would suddenly declaim in the middle of a speech, "and I don't know how to deliver a sermon. All I know how to do is to deliver to you what I have lived." The listener immediately receives the impression that his words are genuine. Rarely can recorded lessons be found that are so free of the desire to impress, persuade, criticize, or moralize. His speeches are generally devoid of a planned structure. Methodology, categories, and organization can be found in his books; but his talks most closely resemble those loose and casual conversations we find in the records of the desert fathers. "Give us a word" was the common salutation with which a company of visitors would greet St. Antony the Great.

Sermonizing was never made a regular part of Abba Matta's leadership as abbot. If there was a special occasion, if there were visitors, if the monks just wanted to sit one evening and hear spiritual words, then the eloquent teacher would sit and share with them his thoughts. His style was always smooth and serene, a natural stream of reflections pouring forth from his heart. Nor could Abba Matta thunder rebukes; "fire and brimstone" was foreign to him; neither did he enjoy discussing the miseries of those who rejected salvation. Such things did not belong to him. He was content instead to contemplate the beauty of Christ, to extol the splendor of Scripture, to enlarge on the joy of the faith, and to ask why, oh why, did not all his listeners feel the blessedness of the Christian life as much as he did?

There is a fine peculiarity to Abba Matta's discourses that most listeners will notice: one can hear the same talk over and over without growing weary. He does not present a set of moral points but instead tells a story. One might occasionally identify in his speeches a dramatic scheme: setting, crescendo, climax, denouement. But what makes his teaching especially valuable is the direct and personal inspiration he communicates to the hearer. He speaks to the heart; he speaks to the mind; he speaks to the body; he speaks to the will; he speaks to the conscience; and he speaks to the imagination. No aspect of human life is left out of his addresses. His words give the impression of a man who was gifted with a boundless imagination, boundless faith, and a boundless love for God.

Finally, it is the hope and prayer of the translator that the first experiences of joy that filled his heart while listening to these Spirit-anointed words during the early days of his youth may also be the experience of the reader. We offer forth these spiritual discourses as a true labor of love, in the hope that they will be received by man as a valuable source of edification, and by God as a perpetual doxology.

—the Translator
The Holy Fifty Days of the Resurrection, 2012

PART I

Spirituality

Repentance and Holiness

1987

Let me begin with the story of the Queen of Sheba.[1] She undoubtedly was a person who was satisfied with herself; but one day, she heard of the king of a country called Israel, a renowned man of God who spoke divine wisdom. She said to herself, "How I long to hear about spiritual things. . . . I am so tired of mere luxury and palaces!" So she mounted her camel and made the month-long journey to Jerusalem. She met with Solomon and asked every question that was on her heart about God and life; and he offered her sound teaching that prompted her to repent. Christ says that the Queen of Sheba will come in the last day to judge each one of us[2]— one who did nothing more than to go on a journey to hear Solomon's wisdom!

Christ says, "Yes, and I came to you with heavenly wisdom, expressed in the simplest manner." The teachings of Christ are not the type of wisdom boasted of by worldly philosophy; rather, Christ's wisdom

---

1   1 Kin 10
2   Matt 12:42

is housed in very simple words. "Love your neighbor as yourself"—scholars can spend a lifetime writing complicated books about such phrases, discussing them in their colleges, and awarding doctor of divinity degrees. But it is only a few short words. The question is *how* to love? Who can achieve such an ideal? Many have done it, for the commandment requires not a large intellect, but a large heart and abundant courage.

A distinguished woman from one of the most eminent families in Egypt once came here (she had never stepped into a monastery before) weeping for her daughter. She approached me with swollen, red eyes requesting confession. She said, "I have an only daughter who is going down the wrong path. She is my only hope in this world, and if she ends up in the wrong place, I will kill myself, and my family's reputation will be destroyed."

I silently prayed within myself, "What can I possibly do, O Lord?" I had a feeling that she was here to expiate her guilt (I don't know if you will understand my meaning); her daughter was turning out bad, so she wished to mitigate her responsibility. So I asked her, "Are you ready to repent?"

She replied, "I'm speaking to you about my daughter."

I said, "But I'm speaking about *you*."

She asked, "What do you mean?"

I told her, "I don't have much to say, because my comments are terse and direct. I only ask you, are you ready to repent?"

She looked at the ground and finally understood, and she wept. "Please tell me how."

I asked her, "Do you believe in the Lord Jesus?"

She said, "I believe, but help my faith."

I told her, "Faith in Christ is a very great thing. To believe in Him is the grandest act."

"Oh, please tell me how to have faith in Christ, and I will do it!"

I told her, "If you believe in Christ, not only will you be saved, but your daughter will return to you."

She said, "Then tell me how!"

I responded, "How can I explain faith in Christ? It's like this: imagine you're standing on the third story of a building, and I am on the ground and say to you, 'Jump!' Would you? I don't think so. But now put Christ in my place, and He tells you, 'Jump!' as He's standing below with open arms. Would you?"

She just gazed at me in amazement, then began to think deeply about it until she grasped the significance of the concept. "I would jump!"

Faith transcends logic. When we follow Christ, we're no longer limited by our thinking and calculations. Two and two do not necessarily make four, but can make eight, ten, or a thousand in Him. "But I don't have enough money in my pocket to feed my wife and children. Will you just tell me, 'Believe in God'?"

Yes, I will tell you to believe in God. The man who does so will find enough money and to spare to feed his family. These are not mere words I am saying; these aren't mere empty theories! These are actual events I've witnessed during my lifetime, as well as circumstances in the lives of my confessors, who have been through the most extraordinary experiences.

Let us return to our lady. I told her, "Look, if you go back to your house, remain in your own room and stop going out everywhere, and take hold of your Bible and pray, your daughter will forsake her path and return to you."

She said, "Are you sure?"

I answered, "On my life."

She went back home, took her Bible, and began a genuinely spiritual life. She had never read her Bible before. She had been all about parties and entertainment, and naturally her daughter turned out like her; from where else could the girl get her behavior? She just took her mother's behavior to the extreme, and one error followed another.

Well, one day while her mother was in her room, the girl came knocking but without answer; she then entered and found her mother with red eyes. "What are you doing, Mother?"

"Nothing, my daughter."

The girl found a Bible in sight and realized her mother must have been praying. She began spying on her; and after a week, the girl came to her mother weeping and threw herself into her arms, saying, "Mother, I want to live like you! I want to repent like you!"

She responded, "I have nothing to do with you. Repent on your own."

This was from my direction; I had told her, "Do not speak a word to her. Leave her to Christ, and He will be able to pull her in; but you won't be able to."

The girl threw away her (what is it called?) miniskirt and sat looking for a long time among her mother's clothes until she found a long dress that reached a ways below the knees; and she went to the church, confessed, and took Communion.

The mother came back to me beaming with joy, saying, "It happened, Abouna; the miracle really happened!"

Yes, it happened; why shouldn't it? And it happened without any strife, and without following any formula or any laws. The mother repents, the daughter repents. The father repents, the whole family repents. The priest lives a good life, the entire church lives a life of repentance. That is how it goes. The king of Nineveh repented, then the whole city repented—and God had mercy on Nineveh, a city that has become an example to the world for all generations.

Beloved, the message of the Gospel is very simple, and its words can be understood without any sermonizing. Some of the abbas once came and told me, "There are some people waiting for you outside; please go give them a short sermon." O people, the Gospel doesn't need sermons! It is never my intention to sermonize, and right now I am not giving you a sermon; I am just bequeathing to you the Gospel's message. Can't you all receive the scriptures as simply as I am delivering them to you now? Have I spoken difficult words? Have I taught philosophically? Never! Christ's words are extremely simple and straightforward. He said, "An evil generation seeks after a sign."[3] But how could they ask for a sign when Christ Himself was present with them! *He* is the sign! He gave life to the dead! For whom was the story of Lazarus recorded? For Lazarus himself? For a past generation? It was recorded *for us*. Lazarus was raised *for me*.

When I first became a monk, I prayed, "See, Lord, I am Your Lazarus. I am lying here in the tomb. Will You raise me up? I am a dead man, and I only ask You to bring me out of this tomb." I kept praying this for a while, twenty-eight days to be exact. Lazarus remained inside for three days, but I remained twenty-eight days in tears, crying out to God, "I am the new Lazarus! Raise me!" At the end of the twenty-eight days, I felt filled with an extraordinary strength, which raised me up in the same way it would raise a dead man from the grave. "Loose him and let him go."[4] I felt finally "loosed" from the world and from all people, from everything, and went forth like Lazarus risen from the dead. It was an experience I could never forget. Those twenty-eight days were the beginning of a new life with God.

When Christ told Lazarus to rise, the command was not just for Lazarus. He was commanding you, every one of us, who are all as Lazarus was. And He can raise you with just a word—if you are willing. Martha wept and said to Him, "If only You were here, my brother would not have died."[5] Oh, really? But Christ was standing right before

---

3 Matt 16:4
4 John 11:44
5 John 11:21

you, Martha. It was an admirable faith that she had, but too little of it. "If You were here three days ago he would not have died"—"Well, I am here now, and I can raise him." He also wants *us* to take this leap from one level of faith to the next; and this is why the story was written. It was never meant to be a mere tale added to the Gospel. They said to Him at the first, "Lord, he whom You love is sick."[6] If He had gone immediately, He would have simply cured him. But He purposely waited till death, that He might show that He not only cures disease, but also raises the dead! He not only heals the broken and wounded soul of man, but He also saves the soul that is caught in the deepest sins of death. He raises it to new life.

In other words, if a man is following a sinful path, but returns to Christ, it's like he just came out of his mother's womb. He's like a firstborn son again, as the priest says, "Receive, O Lord, your firstborn son so-and-so." In precisely the same way (God knows), after repentance, and the return to Christ's bosom, and the tears that wash away sin, and after the sinner hears from Christ's own mouth, "Lazarus, come forth," he rises from the grave of spiritual death, like a newborn emerging from its mother's womb, or like a new soul emerging from the Church's womb in baptism. And if it were a former virgin who lost everything to sin, once she returns to Christ, she returns as one just emerging from the newness of baptism, or as a pure virgin baby first coming out of the womb.

Christ raises men from the dead. And He can raise a person after an hour, or after two days, or more, according to the testimony of Lazarus's sister: "By now there's a stench; do not embarrass us! If we remove the stone, we will all be struck with horror. This is our own brother. His body is decayed, and we won't be able to bear it." But then—"Lazarus, come forth!" I said to that woman, "Only jump from the third story, and Christ will catch you in His arms."

---

6   John 11:3

It need not always require us to jump from the third story; but I made faith appear to this woman like a striking and fearful thing, so that she might tremble and repent. However, I do not want to scare you all today. We are not asked to jump from even the second or first story now, for (God knows!) Christ is standing right behind the door: "Behold, I stand at the door and knock. Whoever hears My voice and opens, I will enter and dine with him."[7] This means, "I will eat from the plate of his pains, and I will participate in his grief." For what else do we have to offer Him? He knocks at the door, I open to Him and say, "Please come in," and then what have I to give Him? I only have the plate of my afflictions and the dish of all my life's problems, which I am incapable of untangling. He will dine with me, and *I will dine with Him*—meaning *He* has something to offer *me*, and you know what good things He gives. Indeed, I do not need to jump from the third or even the second story, but only to open the door. Is it difficult for us to open our hearts to Christ?

There is something I would like to end this point with, for the Gospel ends this passage with it. After Christ spoke of Nineveh and repentance, He said this: "The lamp of the body is the eye." It maybe seems like a strange transition, almost unrelated, but only to the careless reader. "If your eye is simple, your whole body will be luminous; but if it is evil, then your whole body will be darkened. Therefore take heed lest your body be full of darkness."[8] Extraordinary words! This is spoken for us all. The lamp which lightens up the entire chamber within you is the eye. I desire a simple eye! Who doesn't?

The frequent complaint among you in fact is that the eye is not simple and the body is darkened.

When I was young, my eye was what I would call "natural." And one day it was *not* simple, and it erred. I was walking along the beach

---

7   Rev 3:20
8   Matt 6:22, 23

in Alexandria as a youth when my eye faltered, and I was dismayed. The fault terrified me! I felt as if something completely wrong had penetrated my being. I returned to my room and prayed, "See now, Lord, I wish to live only for You. If I spend the rest of my days with my eye wandering this way and that, then I will be a lost soul anyway, and there will be no point in my struggling for anything, praying, going to church, or taking Communion. I implore and beseech You to grant me the simple eye this very moment!" Afterward my experience in this area grew, and I began to understand the significance of the simple eye.

So, what is the simple eye? It is the eye, beloved, that does not desire. It is the eye that perceives without bringing the outside world inside. Woe to the eye that is open to all images around it and internalizes them! You will respond, "So should I walk around with my eyes closed?" Not at all. The simple eye is that which has become satisfied with the good things given to it by God, and is content with the inward gifts of Christ. It allows nothing harmful to enter the heart and fester. But the eye that has no guide or restraint we deem to be not simple. It constantly gives entrance to impurities, and so the body is constantly polluted and darkened.

Again, how can the eye become simple? "My soul has said, 'The Lord is my portion.'"[9]

The layman may say, "What an easy verse for a monk to cite! You're a monk, but I live in the world. Do you want me to also become a monk and walk the streets in black garb?"

But I will answer him, "Believe me, I look upon the world more favorably than do you; and I honor everything in the world more than you do; and I understand everything in the world more than you do."

How? You see, beloved, the person who is satisfied in the Lord is not deprived of anything in this world; he who receives Christ within him misses nothing in the world. This erroneous idea has always been

---

9   Lam 3:24

around, that the follower of Christ is deprived of pleasurable things, and so it's better not to be His follower. "If I become the type who reads the Bible and listens to sermons, I won't be able to go to the cinema, or stay late at parties, or do anything fun. I might as well become a monk!" Completely wrong. The truth is the very opposite.

Let me give you an example. Since the monk never gets married, it's commonly thought that monks don't like kids. But this is false. The fact is that after we forsook the world, marriage, and childbearing, we found the whole world along with everything in it given to us. Let me pose this question to the layman who has a family. Say you have a delightful bunch of little sons and daughters; and your neighbor also has a delightful little bunch of kids, but they are slightly more attractive and more intelligent. Your kids are moderately successful in school, but your neighbor's kids are very successful. What happens? The result is that you can't stand to be around your neighbor; and when your eyes fall on his kids, you immediately look the other way. You become filled with envy and spite, and you can't even stand yourself.

Thus is ownership in the world. When you have something, it owns you rather than you owning it. If a man owns a field that barely raises a crop, and the man next to him owns a slightly bigger field that produces richly, God help the first man! He walks by the second man's field, looking at the lively crop, and the tears begin to fall. Envy and bitterness enter the soul, and he starts complaining, "Woe is me! Why is this happening, O Lord?" and he may even blaspheme. The problem is that, when he bought the field, the field actually bought him. He did not become the owner of the field, but the field swallowed him up. So you see that worldly possession, my beloved, turns around and possesses us.

The man who has an extra thousand dollars may seem happy with his surplus, but instead he sits and nervously counts it. He then obsesses about how he can get a little more, so he decides to put in extra hours after work, though his health is feeble, and his children sit waiting for him till late at night—all for the sake of a few extra dollars. The man who has a million dollars may seem quite content and free of envy. But no! He stares unhappily at the man who has two million. So he stresses himself in dealings with the bank, in investments, and yells at his employees, all for the sake of more money. He finishes his work and gets home by 10 PM, then sits from 10 PM to midnight calculating his profits in his mind. Now go to that man and say, "What about the Bible?" and he will answer "Bible? You think I have time for that?"

Even if Christ asked him about his Bible, he would say, "I'm a man of business; I have no time for it."

But then Christ would respond, "But I gave you this money so that you might return to Me what is mine. The Old Testament clearly states My right to a tenth."[10] What is a tenth of twenty-four hours? About two and a half hours—this is the official tithe of your daily time.

The businessman will retort, "I have my work and obligations to handle. I'm swamped all day at work. Just come and see for yourself! When I get home I need to relax."

Christ will say, "Get up, or I'll take back the money I gave you."

God knows that the story I'm about to tell you is true, and I tell it not just for you but for everyone who is listening to me now. I once knew a businessman who said in my hearing, "If poverty chased me with an airplane it would never catch up to me. I'm so-and-so! Poverty can never touch me." This man was a neighbor of mine in a certain city, and he was extremely wealthy. He would invite pashas to his home for dinner, and everyone knew to render him a special level of honor to avoid offending him. He was a Muslim, but he and his son were my friends.

One day, his son came to me dressed in black, saying, "My father is dead."

---

10   Lev 27:30

"Really?" I asked.

He answered yes, but his face displayed unusual signs. I asked him how it happened, but his mind was in another place. He finally admitted something he could no longer withhold: "I want to tell you something, but please keep it a strict secret." I answered, of course I would.

"You see," he continued, "my father is not actually dead. He entered into a disastrous business deal and is ruined. He had to sell all his assets; all his real estate has been seized, and he's fled from the city. He escaped in the middle of the night. The authorities confronted the family and threw us all out of our home."

"Could it be?" I said.

"Yes. It all happened this month."

My God! This was the man who said, "If poverty chased me with an airplane it would not catch me."

Four or five months after that, the son came back to me and desired to tell me something else. "I received news from the police that they found my father dead. He had his wallet with him, and they immediately identified him because of his wide reputation; so they immediately contacted us."

"Where did they find him?" I asked. He said that the poor man was carrying a box of chickens, because he was reduced to selling chickens to survive; and since he couldn't bear himself, he died.

Christ tells us, "Your money really belongs to Me. Your youth is Mine, and I can take it back from you tomorrow. I even have a claim on your health; if you do not offer it to Me, I can withdraw it. The glory you enjoy is actually Mine; if you do not render it to Me, I will take the other nine-tenths of it from you, and even the tithe you held back will be seized." Christ was sorely distressed because of this, and He said, "The Queen of the South will rise up and judge this generation," because they refused to heed Him. The judgment awaits! God is not lying—He can never say something and then go back on His word later. I may be frightening you now, but I am compelled to because this is the Gospel's message.

Let me go back to the simple eye to conclude my remarks. Even if a man has millions of dollars, and yet has devoted his life and heart to God, nothing at all can separate him from Christ. He would indeed be willing to forsake all for Christ's sake. Is it difficult for a man to sell everything and follow Christ? No, for the "selling" is inward. Have you sold everything or not? There are those who are outwardly rich but have inwardly sold everything and abandoned all for Christ. There is also the man who has outwardly sold everything—the monk—but inwardly he has not. For he still hankers after the world, and position, and honor. Has such a one sold everything? No. Has such a one the simple eye? No.

The simple eye is that which has dispensed with possession; ownership no longer owns it. Woe to the man who is owned by his money! Woe to the woman who is owned by her beauty! Woe to the person who is owned by his own health and abilities! God gives us good health, and we abuse it. God gives us money, and we grow arrogant. What then, brethren?

Every one of you must determine what abilities he's been given and submit them to Christ, before he is found at fault. Believe me, every young man or woman who offers his or her youth to Christ will never grow old. Every person who offers his strength to Christ will never grow weak. Every rich person who has given his riches to Christ has never become poor. Christ is a great surety for our personal "assets," but sadly we have not known Him enough. And this lack of knowledge in man always leads to Christ's rebuke—"Woe to you, scribes and Pharisees!"

When God's anger falls upon man, it's a severe thing. But God wants what's on our inside, not what's on the outside. We have grown accustomed to giving God only our exterior, but today we need to reverse that—forget about appearances, forget about outward forms! God desires the heart; He desires the inward life.

And I may end today's word with this: The lamp of the body is the eye. If your eye is simple, your whole body—and your whole life—will be luminous. No darkness shall remain.

Glory be to God in His Church forever, amen.

On the Faith of the Believer

1973

Today's Gospel, my beloved, is very important to every soul.[1] The Lord revealed Himself in many ways to the Jews, but as the Prophet Isaiah said, "They have closed their ears and their eyes, lest they hear with their ears and see with their eyes, and come to Me and be healed."[2] They rejected the Lord at the time when they were in need of accepting Him; and we have done the same. The Lord comes often to knock on the heart's door and reveal Himself, but we ignore His voice and close up our hearts to the Holy Spirit; and so the Lord leaves. There is an acceptable time and an hour of salvation; but if we refuse that time and that hour, we are deprived of that incredible gift—that the Lord would hear us.

"I am going away. And you will seek me, but you will die in your sins. Where I go you cannot follow."[3]

Strange words, Lord! You Yourself said, "I will be with you always,

---

1   The Gospel passage was taken from John 8.
2   Is 6:10
3   John 8:21

even unto the end of the ages."[4] How then can You say, "Where I go you cannot follow"? Beloved, the Lord is truly present; but He is not present in every heart. It is for this reason that I am speaking with you this morning, and this is why this Gospel passage is written. The Lord indeed might be present in the person sitting on your right or left, sitting in front or behind you, but not in you yourself. How can you beseech Him, and how can He hear you, if you do not *own* Him? Beloved, the words, "Where I go you cannot follow," indicate a deep rift, an unbridgeable chasm, between those who seek God in the acceptable time and those who have shut up their hearts to the Spirit's voice.

So the Jews said, "Will He kill Himself, because He said, 'Where I go you cannot follow'?"[5] Christ's response is very important: "You are from beneath; I am from above. I go unto My Father; and you will seek Me but not find Me. . . . The chosen will see Me; but you will not see Me. . . . I said to you that you will die in your sins, because you do not believe that I am He."[6] They said to Him, "Who are You?"

The original language clarifies the dialogue. Remember when Moses asked about God's name, He said, "I AM."[7] In the Septuagint this reads as *ego eimi*, which means, "I am the self-existent." Christ repeats the same words Moses heard from God: "You do not believe that *ego eimi* [I AM]." He uses the expression that no one can use except Jehovah. The Arabic is lacking, so forgive me if I return to the original language; but I must show you the importance of these words. When Christ therefore says, "You will die in your sins, because you do not believe that I AM," His meaning is quite clear to them.

They said, "Who do You make Yourself out to be?"

He answered, "I am He who spoke to You from the beginning."[8]

---

4   Matt 28:20
5   John 8:22
6   John 8:23–25
7   Ex 3:14
8   John 8:25

I would like to stop here and ask, "Do we, beloved, believe that Christ is the I AM?" I ask You, Lord, that You would never forsake us on account of the weakness of our faith! Grant us vigilant hearts, enlightened minds, eyes to see, and ears to hear Your voice in the acceptable time and in the hour of salvation.

So the work that will have a vast impact on our lives is to believe in Christ—*as Christ* and as no one else. It's as He once asked His disciples, "Who do men say that I am?"[9]

They said Elijah, or Jeremiah, or one of the prophets.

"But who do you say that I am?"

They said, "You are the Christ, the Son of God," and for this Christ rejoiced. Whenever Christ encountered a strong faith, He would exult and rejoice greatly; but whenever He met with weak faith, He would be severely grieved.

Last Friday we spoke about the Canaanite woman[10] who worshipped Baal. This woman, who had the benefit of neither the law, nor rites, nor priest, nor sacrifice, went to Christ and said, "Heal my daughter," and received her request.

The chapter before that tells of the disciples as they crossed the sea in a boat and how Christ came to them walking on the water. Peter said, "Lord, if it's You,"—notice the *if*; isn't that something?—"if it's You, command me to come to You on the water."

So whereas to the Canaanitess He said, "O woman, great is your faith," to Peter, who saw the violent winds and sank, He said, "O you of little faith, why did you doubt?" How grieved was Christ! This was Peter, His own disciple, who had heard Him teach for so long, who ultimately sank. What a sad contrast is drawn between Peter's faith and the Canaanite woman's!

In this way did Christ always sense the inner faith of the hearer,

---

9   Matt 16:13
10   See "On the Canaanite Woman," page 121.

just as God also senses the faith in every heart among us. In the early Church, the people were called "the faithful." What a lovely name! This is the consummation of life and of religion. Let us consider the criteria for this appellation and if indeed we qualify. Recall the story of the Ethiopian and Philip, who was carried by the Spirit.[11] The Ethiopian asked him, "Here is some water. Can I be baptized?" And Philip's reply: "If you believe with *all your heart*." Oh, see the loftiness of faith required for the mysteries!

Beloved, do we believe in Christ with all our hearts? Paul—a good man, whom I love dearly—received many good qualities from Christ, and faith determined the tenor of his heart. In the first chapter of Romans he says, "I thank my God in Christ Jesus that your faith is spoken of throughout the world".[12] Faith is the ultimate goal of every evangelist, and it is faith that made Paul's heart throb. When he found one of his churches full of faith, he would rejoice.

O God, should I myself rejoice in those sitting before me? Is there in our hearts, O Lord, a real faith that is worthy of You? These are simply questions I throw out to God and to you all, that I may stir up your hearts. Does the faith within you fill the entire heart? Is it a faith that would make Paul glad? Is your faith large enough to hold all the graces you received in Baptism, Communion, and the rest of the mysteries? Many people ask, "Abba, why is it that we take Communion, then return to sin?" Or, "Abba, aren't we baptized, and don't we have the Holy Spirit in our hearts?" Yes—but our faith is not from all our hearts!

Again, I admire the Apostle Paul for his enormous faith in Christ. The power that nourished Paul's heart—and will nourish yours—was derived from the Cross. Beloved, I am not "preaching," because I am not a preacher. My duty is simply to take a soul by the hand and guide it step by step to the heart of Christ. Will you help me? Paul: you know

---

11   Acts 8
12   Rom 1:8

what kind of man he was from his epistles. He carried the Gentiles on his shoulders and offered to Christ an innumerable multitude of souls, without ever seeing Christ in the flesh. He looked unto the profound love of Christ, and to what end that love ultimately led: that colossal heart drained itself until its life was completely poured out, and He bowed His head upon the Cross.

Then Paul wrote a verse which must be memorized by every person: "I was crucified with Christ."[13] Ah, no one else had said it before him! O Paul, who taught you this? It wasn't written in the Scriptures, and nobody had told it to you! Did you receive it from Peter? Did you receive it from any of the pillars of the Church?[14] Oh, who gave you this truth? The Lord! And see what follows: "It is not I who live, but Christ who lives in me." Implant this verse into your hearts—all of it—all, I say! He continues: "The life which I now live in the flesh, I live by *faith*"—there it is—"I live by faith in the Son of God, who loved me and gave Himself up for me." Beloved, Christ said that faith moves mountains; but you have not received the mountain's measure of faith but rather the measure of a mustard seed.[15] My job today is to give to you at least a mustard seed's amount of faith. Is it enough? Brethren, I am imparting to you the spring of faith that will allow you to dwell in Christ, or rather, Christ to dwell in you.

"'If you do not believe that I AM, you will die in your sins.' Then they said to Him, 'Who are You?'" But they asked without wanting to learn anything. There are people today who likewise ask without wishing to learn, who come to me and say, "May we speak with you?" Then I hear a litany of questions, all theoretical and pointless, without any trace of a desire to improve their faith or life. I lament and my throat goes dry, because I don't know how to engage in theoretical debates; all I

---

13 Gal 2:20
14 Gal 2:9
15 Matt 17:20

know how to do is to give others what I have lived. We can thank the Pharisees, in any event, for their spiteful question, because it elicited an edifying and powerful response. "Jesus said to them, 'I am the one who has spoken to you from the beginning.'" Ah, we're about to receive good things from these words! O Lord Jesus, what is it that You said from the beginning?

Notice what Christ said to Nathanael in St. John's Gospel: "From now on you will see heaven opened and the angels of God ascending and descending upon the Son of Man."[16] My Lord, what is there in this vision for us? What else, but that the Lord Jesus is the ladder that links heaven to earth! He is the ladder who said, "I am the Way." But what if the ladder were removed? Could anyone ascend? This is the first truth Christ ever uttered about Himself. It is not a small thing, for without Him none of us can go up. We must all say, "Lord, without You, my life has no worth!" Why? Because it would begin from the earth and end in the earth. It's one hundred percent certain that whoever does not have Christ and does not believe in Him will not ascend. Rather, he will die and return to the earth from which he was taken.

Christ said much more, but I don't think the time will suffice us. Let us move on. He afterward spoke with Nicodemus regarding a critical issue. He told him, "You must be born from above."[17] I believe the issue is now becoming clearer.

Nicodemus asked, "Can a man re-enter his mother's womb?"

He answered, "Are you the teacher of Israel and do not know? For it is written, 'You are My Son, and today I have begotten You.'"[18] That is, "You're the teacher of Israel, and have the Psalms memorized, and do not understand?" This is a rebuke to those who memorize the Psalms but do not know how to apply them.

---

16   John 1:51
17   John 3:3, alternate translation
18   Ps 2:7

Then Christ said, "Just as Moses lifted up the serpent in the wilderness, so must the Son of Man must be lifted up."[19] So, Lord Jesus, just as those who were bitten by serpents were healed by looking to the brazen serpent, will it be the same with You? "Yes. Look unto Me and you will be saved."[20] Brethren, we are all bitten! The serpent has injured us all, and the poison courses through our veins. Who does not run after the desires of the flesh? Who can control his eyes from morning to night? Who, just who, when we are all bitten? But Christ was lifted up to heal the death within us, to purge the poison of sin, and to break the scorpion's tail. The poison will be drained, and we will be healed by His Blood.

Let us consider another matter. Christ said to Peter, "O you of little faith," but to the Canaanite woman, "O you of great faith." But what was the *standard* by which the one faith was judged "little" and the other "great"? Or what were the two faiths measured against? The standard was Christ Himself. Christ said to Peter, "I'm here right before you, and you doubted?" His faith could not reach to the Christ standing directly before him; and so he drowned. Ah, my Lord Jesus, I fear lest our faith not reach You! But that is why we drown every day. The Canaanite woman, on the other hand, had no religion or rites to support her heart, but was able to gain the faith which reaches to the level of Christ. She focused all her faith on Christ: "I can't, but You can."

Today I am revealing to you what you will say to the Lord in your prayers. You will say, "I am the new Canaanitess. I have nothing to justify myself. But hear, O Lord God! You taught us in the story of the Canaanite woman that You can be prevailed upon; so I am hear to prevail upon You by my faith. You will heal me!"

Or the priest would say, "You will strengthen my church! I cannot

---

19 John 3:14
20 Is 45:22

preach to a dead people. I cannot speak to a generation dominated by Satan." Satan had possessed the Canaanitess's daughter, and he is controlling the young men and women of the Church who are out wandering in the streets. The priest must say to the Lord, "My people are possessed! Do not dismiss me from before Your altar until I receive a promise that You will give a new spirit to this people. Eliminate Satan's authority by which he has deluded my children and caused their ears not to hear and their eyes not to see! I am not only beseeching you, but I am wrestling with You; for You taught us to do so in the Gospel of the Canaanite woman."

Christ knocks at the door, He is knocking even now, and He waits patiently and humbly to enter. He doesn't grow angry but waits a very long time. I once sent a letter to someone who was going astray in the world, saying, "Repent, lest you lose heaven for the sake of silly and trivial things of earth! My son, I beg of you, do not waste your young life on dead things! When you advance in age, you will find them utterly worthless, and they will die in your hands and to your heart. Do not sell the Kingdom for fleeting nonsense!"

He wrote to me, saying, "I know all about the Kingdom and about Christ, but I will never meet with either, so leave me alone."

My God above! I wrote back, "Take heed! If you seek to repent hereafter, the chance will be gone."

At length he responded, "I have realized that I sinned a great sin, and I am prepared to repent." So, beloved, does the Lord knock at the door—but not forever!

Do we enjoy the presence of Christ? I don't just mean reading the Bible, but experiencing a direct link with Christ every day. Christ is with me at home, on the road, at work, at my service, at the altar. Brethren, do we receive that mystical life of Christ by daily prayers, by tears, by entreaties, by striking the breast, by constant kneeling, by the Word, by the heavenly bread placed upon the spiritual table? Ah, our

Lord Jesus Christ, grant us the living water and the Blood to drink, which having drunk, we will not thirst again after sin! "Remember your Creator in the days of your youth, before the days come when you say, 'I have no pleasure in them.'"[21] The days are certainly coming when you will say, "You speak about repentance, Abba, but how can I repent? I can't fast because of my sickness. I can't kneel because of my rheumatism. My back, knees, and bowels are all problematic. Abba, I have ten to twelve diseases!" That is why today I say, remember your Creator. Hold to the Cross, eat and drink spiritual things, before the time comes when your appetite is blunted! At that time you will not be able to eat, even if the food is placed right in front of you.

Yesterday someone was telling me, "Abba, you talk to us about the Bible, but I can't even open it. I just can't. Do you have a remedy?"

I told him, "Ah, there's a certain sin binding the heart and restraining the soul from the word of life. You might or might not know what it is." I looked in his eyes and saw them flicker. He knew it very well! I said, "Have you figured it out?"

He said, "Yes, I have."

O beloved, sin is malignant, causing the altar itself to be tasteless to us and forcing us to avoid it. It makes the Bible heavy on the digestion. We read just two lines and begin yawning in disinterest.

I conclude my words by saying that the Bible is open before you, along with all the words spoken by Christ. It is all power, all a gift, given to the soul; it is faith itself poured as living water into the mouth of the thirsty. The drinker is refreshed and exclaims, "Ah, how cool and wonderful is this water!" Beloved, it is the same with the word of life, when it abides in the heart of an attentive believer. "If anyone thirsts, let him come to Me."[22] O Lord Jesus Christ, quench our thirst by Your own hand! Grant every soul to remember its true thirst for You, that

21 Eccl 12:1
22 John 7:37

it would drink and be refreshed, and not thirst again for this world and its sin. Our living God, satisfy the hearts of your servants today. Amen. May Your name be glorified.

Living in the Flesh
versus Living in the Spirit

1976

There is therefore now no condemnation to those who are in Christ Jesus, who do not walk according to the flesh, but according to the Spirit. For the law of the Spirit of life in Christ Jesus has made me free from the law of sin and death. For what the law could not do in that it was weak through the flesh, God did by sending His own Son in the likeness of sinful flesh, on account of sin: He condemned sin in the flesh, that the righteous requirement of the law might be fulfilled in us who do not walk according to the flesh but according to the Spirit. For those who live according to the flesh set their minds on the things of the flesh, but those who live according to the Spirit, the things of the Spirit. For to be carnally minded is death, but to be spiritually minded is life and peace. Because the carnal mind is enmity against God; for it is not subject to the law of God, nor indeed can be. So then, those who are in the flesh cannot please God.

But you are not in the flesh but in the Spirit, if indeed the Spirit of God dwells in you. Now if anyone does not have the Spirit of Christ, he is not His. And if Christ is in you, the body is dead because of sin, but the Spirit is life because of righteousness. But if the Spirit of Him who raised Jesus from the dead dwells in you, He who raised Christ from the dead will also give life to your mortal bodies through His Spirit who dwells in you. Therefore, brethren, we are debtors—not to the flesh, to live according to the flesh. For if you live according to the flesh you will die; but if by the Spirit you put to death the deeds of the body, you will live. (Rom. 8:1–13, NKJV)

I have found that human nature can be divided into three different stages or orders regarding our life with God. The Bible has revealed them in very clear terms without, however, forcing them into a "system." A major fault of this generation is that it attempts to force the simple and free teachings of the Bible into schemes to be analyzed and committed to rote memorization. I consider it a fault because it was always the Spirit's work to grant these things to man; but because of our spiritual weakness, we are compelled to overwork the mind in order to compensate for our spiritual deficiencies.

The Bible expresses the three orders of man in various places, and they are, first, the *natural* man; second, the *carnal* man; and third, the *spiritual* man. These three orders are not strictly confined; every person passes through each of them. And there are times when a person can be at the zenith of the spiritual life but still backslide, if even just for a moment, and look upon God's things as if they were foolish. So let us see where we stand among these three orders and find what is required of us to do.

The *natural* man was described by the Apostle Paul as he who does not accept the things of God.[1] Everything divine is rejected by him;

---

1   1 Cor 2:14

and the rejection is not due to stubbornness or ignorance but rather to his sheer incapability to receive them. He simply lacks the capacity. Talk to him about God, and he doesn't understand. Talk to him about salvation and eternal life, and he is completely lost. Talk to him about the Bible, and he won't see the purpose. He will just tell you, "Do you really believe all this babble?"

The best description of the *carnal* man is found in Romans 7. He is a person who, although he knows God and His laws very well, attends church, is a member of the choir, and has a keen knowledge of dogma and theology, yet nevertheless lives according to the flesh. The flesh wields authority over him. In a few short sentences St. Paul gives a profound and splendid picture of him by describing the state he himself was in before believing in Christ, as well as the remnants of that state which lingered on in him. Paul was extremely honest in speaking about his own life and faithfully included every detail, so that they who found themselves in a similar state could find hope and salvation. He says:

> For we know that the law is spiritual, but I am carnal, sold under sin. For what I am doing, I do not understand. For what I will to do, that I do not practice; but what I hate, that I do. If, then, I do what I will not to do, I agree with the law that it is good. But now, it is no longer I who do it, but sin that dwells in me. For I know that in me (that is, in my flesh) nothing good dwells; for to will is present with me, but how to perform what is good I do not find. For the good that I will to do, I do not do; but the evil I will not to do, that I practice. Now if I do what I will not to do, it is no longer I who do it, but sin that dwells in me. I find then a law, that evil is present with me, the one who wills to do good. For I delight in the law of God according to the inward man. But I see another law in my members, warring against the law of my mind, and bringing me into captivity to the

law of sin which is in my members. O wretched man that I am! Who
will deliver me from this body of death? (Rom. 7:14–24, NKJV)

Such is the carnal man who lives in Christ Jesus. He might know
everything about the Bible and salvation, but his will is not crucified;
and so he does not find how to do good. He is a person whose flesh is
the source of his will. The flesh, that is, holds captive and dictates his
thoughts and behavior. He knows the right thing to do, but his actions
do not reflect what is right; his thoughts lack the grace of the Spirit,
and you cannot detect in his actions the fragrance of Christ.

So I sat to meditate on the Old Testament, because, as you know, it
is my desire to find out how every New Testament teaching is reflected
in the Old. The Old Testament does not have verbal descriptions of the
spiritual orders of man, but it does illustrate them by circumstances
and events. For example, when the people of Israel were in the land of
Egypt, they were a "natural" people, because they did not have the law.
Even when God commanded Moses to deliver them, he asked God,
"But who shall I tell them sent me?"[2] They didn't know God, or His
name, or His ways, or anything about Him at all. Thus Israel in Egypt
can be considered the simplest and best example of the natural man.

Yet they were not rejected by God, but a beloved people, as God
said to Moses: "I have gone down to Egypt because the cry of this
people has come to My ears. I found them in affliction so I resolved to
comfort them."[3] So we see how the natural man, who possesses no law,
has yet a God who still searches for him!

The carnal man is also illustrated by the people of Israel, when they
had left Egypt and were instructed with the words, "Hear, O Israel:
the Lord our God, the Lord is One."[4] These words are the creed of the

---

2   Ex 3:13
3   Ex 3:7, 8
4   Deut 6:4

Old Testament, and they are referred to as the *Shema*. So the people received a creed and learned the name of God, and what is more amazing, they now lived in God's presence. But they wandered forty years in the desert, a lost and carnal people, while God went before them! He was to them a pillar of cloud by day, to shield them from the sun, and a pillar of fire by night, to illuminate the darkness for them. In both cases they were *protected*. But not a week had passed after they crossed the Red Sea when they began to complain to Moses, "How wonderful were the garlic and onions of Egypt compared to this wilderness! Did you bring us out here to kill us? Where is this God of yours?" A fine illustration of how the carnal man thinks! All he wants to do is to eat, drink, and take it easy.

"The people sat to eat and drink and rose up to play."[5] They went from lust for food, to lust for leisure, to lust for adultery, and ended up in idol worship—and they returned again to the golden calf. You see how the carnal man lives by the lusts of the flesh, which eventually leads to apostasy. The people of Israel in the desert measured all things by food and drink; for even when God promised them Canaan, He did not speak of it as a land where there would be a temple, worship, and miracles, but a land "flowing with milk and honey."[6]

I would like to describe this condition using an alternate (though harder) expression: it is the *order of apostasy*. The people were in constant rebellion against God due to their addiction to the lusts of the flesh. It is impossible, beloved, for a person to be addicted to the flesh and still be faithful to God. So God could not transfer the people from the desert to the Promised Land, from the carnal order to the spiritual order, without a process of *sifting*. The only two who entered the land were Joshua and Caleb, for they alone displayed a complete trust in God; and the rest died. It is impossible, brethren, to

---

5   Ex 32:6; 1 Cor 10:7
6   Deut 31:20

pass from the carnal order to the spiritual order without a *death*. God could not bring the Israelites to the Promised Land, which stands for the spiritual order, without first doing away with the carnal element among them.

And so must we die to the things of the flesh. Many tend to question and deliberate—though there is really no deliberation about it—"How can we die to the flesh? How do we ascend from the carnal to the spiritual?" It is only by dying to the flesh. Haven't you ever seen a carnal man accumulate money, sumptuous clothing, food and drink, and store up in abundance everything man could possibly want, until, as the Bible says, a voice came to him: "This night your soul will be taken; so whose will those things be which you have stored up?"[7] The rich man died, and all his possessions vanished. Likewise, beloved, all our desires for possession, pleasures, and ambition must be erased. Nothing less will do. If any bit remains, our advancement from the carnal to the spiritual will not take place.

The Israelites' journey in the desert was significantly prolonged, you see, because the rule of the carnal order persists for a long time; however, the tender mercies of God await our salvation. Never consider God's longsuffering to be due to negligence or forgetfulness; He rather suffers long that we might wake up and understand that we have entered the age of salvation, and that it is a tragedy to spend one more night subject to the carnal order.

But let me say that, even while we live in the flesh and in apostasy, God never forsakes us! The pillar of light never left that people, though twenty-three thousand died in a night due to their sin.[8] God's mercies never leave a sinful man! Jesus pursues you with wounded hands and feet and says, "See, I am still yours. You've sinned so much, but don't forget that I was crucified for you!" By a cloud He shields you from

---

7   Luke 12:20
8   1 Cor 10:8

the heat of day; by kind words He strengthens your heart during the midnight of despair; and by Scripture He comforts you and causes the tears to fall from your eyes.

Let me now illustrate for you the spiritual struggle of the carnal man; and we find a fit analogy in Israel's war with Amalek.[9] The name itself is scary enough.[10] They were a fierce and strong-bodied race, and symbolically they represent the devil and his league. The Israelites were struck with terror, which precisely signifies what happens to the carnal man in spiritual warfare: he *fears*. Then came Moses, symbol of the law, who stood to pray. When he cried out, their success would increase; when he grew weary, their success would wane. And so is the carnal man: always in a bitter struggle, always on the brink of defeat. They brought Hur and Aaron to support Moses' arms while he cried out to God; and the people proceeded to conquer.

The whole picture is of a man whose source of strength is the law and the body, not the spirit. And in times of weakness, when war rises up against him, he fails to overcome. It is a sore experience, and he throws himself into prayers of desperation, just like the Israelites who fought all day and finally vanquished the Amalekite giants late in the night. The Israelites celebrated their victory, but what a poignant bitterness accompanied the win!

Let's now consider Israel after they crossed the Jordan.[11] They journeyed a little and soon ran into Jericho. "What is this Jericho?" they asked.[12]

The response was that it was a mighty fortress, and enemies would soon pour out of the city to devour them.

---

9   Ex 17:8–16

10 In Arabic, *Amalek* indicates "giant."

11 Josh 3

12 In retelling the story of the battle of Jericho, Abba Matta employs his unique and charming style of imagining the conversations that are implied rather than spelled out in the sacred text.

"So what now, Joshua?" they replied. "After all our troubles, have you brought us here to die?"

"No," he responded, "do not be afraid. I feel something special is about to happen. We have entered a new era. We only need to pray."

Joshua here raises the people from a state of apostasy to a state of faith. "So how can we overcome this great city?" they asked. "Should we call for the valiant men and make a collection of weapons?"

"No one will lift a sword," was Joshua's response. "God will be exalted."

How marvelous is the spiritual order! He ordered the priests to prepare themselves with rams' horns, despite the people's probable objections that these things had nothing to do with war; and he ordered the people, without a single shout or noise, to follow the priests around the city. The soldiers of Jericho watched from their summits as the Israelites performed their apparently nonsensical processions, and they ridiculed them as an insane race—and thus are spiritual people often mocked today. This is the warfare of the spiritual order. My Lord, lift me up to this order! Enough of the sword and violence! I've endured the warfare of the carnal man my whole life, O Lord. Brethren, it is imperative that we attain to the spiritual order. The battle is the Lord's. We will find hosts of unseen angels coming to our aid. Every spiritual ear has heard them riding upon the clouds with the sound of thunder in their train.

So it is three different "orders" that we have; and we have spent far too long in the middle one, for the proof of this is the type of warfare we undergo. Can we say that our warfare is of the spiritual order, where we simply declare, "The battle is the Lord's," and find the giants collapse in a moment? According to our theology and traditions, we *are* of the spiritual order. According to names and appearances, that is, we seem spiritual; but according to the nature of our warfare—a stressed, anxious, painful warfare—we are, alas, carnal. Brethren, we live in dire distress, and suffer acute hunger and thirst, because of our standing between two different orders.

There are many of us who complain, "Why am I so lost in my spiritual life? God must have forsaken me because of His displeasure."

No, my friend, not at all! He is constantly shading you by day and lighting your way by night. He only wants to tell you, "Kneel before Me." He waits a long time; and it is not due to His indifference but to His desire that we return to Him. This is a crucial issue in our spiritual lives and a point I keenly desire to correct in your spiritual understanding. When the period of our separation from God is prolonged and our estrangement from Him grows severe, He still waits for our reconciliation! Do you wish to clearly see the mercy of God? Consider your own life, how much you've managed to sin while God silently waits for your repentance. However, despite God's mercy and longsuffering, there still resides real danger in these phases of separation. This is because such phases indicate that the spirit has yielded to the flesh and the will has sunk under the weight of its desires.

Let me turn to another point. I want you to ask yourselves this question: "Shall the flesh dominate me to such an extent that I would choose to please my body and turn a deaf ear to—not the Church or even the Bible—but to the Holy Spirit?" Is my *will* so defeated that I would choose the desires of the flesh over the voice of the Holy Spirit, who tirelessly speaks in me? "If you, by the Spirit, put to death the works of the flesh, you will live."[13]

One of the abbas said to me, "The things you tell us are fine and good, and I understand that I must die to sin. But can you tell me *how* exactly I accomplish this death?"

I told him, "Of course: go up to the fifth story of a building and throw yourself down."

---

13   Rom 8:13

Brethren, obeying the verse which urges us to put to death the desires of the flesh requires the same reckless zeal! No amount of danger or violence should hinder us from mortifying the flesh. We even see kids doing this but in a misguided way. They throw themselves off of Cairo Tower to die, merely because they couldn't finish their bachelor's degree; and, my goodness, do they have such strength of will to kill the body just to avoid appearing as failures before their peers! We all, each one of us, equally have the full and sufficient ability to mortify the flesh.

We will all die one day. There is a death that leads to perdition and a death that leads to eternal life. If we weren't going to die eventually, then all this talk about "mortification" would be a needless gloom. You would certainly say, "This fellow sitting before us and talking about death is a *pessimist*. Get us someone else! We want someone to speak to us smooth words and about pleasant topics, and to say, 'We're all saved, brethren. Hallelujah!'"

No, I won't give you this; but neither am I a pessimist. Here is God's Word, Old and New Testaments, which I set before you; so you judge for yourselves, and may God judge my words before you. Salvation is not easy. Salvation requires a *death*. But if we are all eventually going to die, why not just do it now by our own will? Let us choose the death that leads to eternal life. This is the real victory. And this is the invitation given to us this evening.

There was once a blessed court judge (whose name escapes me) who was pressured to judge a case dishonestly—that is, to pronounce innocent a man whom he knew to be guilty. He tried to extricate himself from the case but was not able. On the day of the trial, instead of going to the courthouse, he threw himself from a rooftop and died. He was a Christian, you see, and simple at heart, and so could not bring himself to declare the false judgment; he could not silence the voice of his conscience. But, one may ask, why not just let the criminal go? He could have just convinced himself that the misdeed was an act of "mercy" and so quieted his conscience. However, his conscience had reached such a point of refinement that he preferred to die rather than to pass false judgment on a man.

This strength to die is present in all of us! I am not requesting of you the death of the body, which is a trivial death; rather, I desire the mortification of the body's *desires*. I want to arouse the capacity, or the "potential," that God placed in your nature to defeat the flesh. Believe me, if God had not given us this potential, the Holy Spirit would never have required us to mortify the fleshly desires.

I can never forget a calculation that was once made regarding the Israelites in the desert. They counted up six hundred thousand men who bore the sword,[14] and according to an average family count of four relatives per one man, it is estimated that about three million Israelites undertook the desert journey. Out of these, only two entered the Promised Land.[15] That gives us a ratio of one individual out of one and a half million. Never forget this number! It reveals the extent to which sin overcomes and masters humanity, as well as how successfully sin makes itself into an idol and pushes God into the dark. So warfare with the flesh is not a light task, as if we could handle it merely by nice thoughts, or as though we could simply say, "Oh yes, I will soon win, God willing." No; I want to make very clear for you the actual, perilous significance of this fight. For the world today seems to be plagued by the same ratio of sin and is not a jot aware of it.

Let's now read from Hebrews. "Therefore, as the Holy Spirit says: 'Today, if you will hear His voice, do not harden your hearts as in the rebellion, in the day of trial in the wilderness, where your fathers tested Me, tried Me, and saw My works forty years. Therefore I was angry with that generation, and said, "They always go astray in their

---

14 Num 1:46
15 Joshua and Caleb.

heart, and they have not known My ways." So I swore in My wrath, "They shall not enter My rest.""[1]

Today God thankfully speaks by His Spirit, and no more as in the days of old, when His voice would descend like thunder upon Moses and the people. It was a fearsome sound that would cause the Israelites' ears to tremble, so that they would all flee from His presence. Let us thank God that today His voice is calm, peaceful, and steals individually into every heart. "Today, if you will hear His voice"—the Holy Spirit's voice—"do not harden your hearts." The consequence resulting from the Israelites' hardening against God's voice was their loss of entering into His rest. So the consequence of spurning the Spirit's voice in our hearts is deprivation of entering into *peace*—even temporal peace. He who turns a deaf ear to any of the Spirit's urgings—to good work, to God's service, to humility, or to anything else—forfeits his peace. What happened to the Israelites in the wilderness was certainly not isolated to their own lives, but as St. Paul says, "These things were written as an example for us."[2]

The Holy Spirit still speaks in each one of us! The Spirit teaches you how to conduct yourself, how to shake off the burdens of your past, how to battle against giants, how to lift up your arms like Moses to defeat the enemy; and God will straightaway fight for you. I have hope in Jesus Christ that He will render these words useful to you, that we might together be able to cross the great chasm that separates the life according to the flesh from the life according to the spirit. I pray that we might pass from the authority and pull of the fleshly desires to submit to the tug of the Holy Spirit. And I pray that we might be filled with power, and grace, and all the gifts that are given us by Christ. Grant us, O Lord, to be victorious by You and to live for You. Amen.

---

1   Heb 3:7–11
2   1 Cor 10:11

On Love

1975

Today we will talk about love. We will read two passages to serve as an introduction to the subject—or better, to empower our souls to love. In truth, when we talk about love, we talk about life itself; for our life is summed up in Christ. The first passage is from the mouth of our Lord.[3] Only the final verse of the chapter mentions the word *love*, but the entire passage is imbued with an exquisite sense of love. This, one of the final prayers offered by Christ on earth, overflows with the finest and most splendid sentiments of love, not only toward the disciples[4] but also toward all those who would believe in Him.[5] These are really the most beautiful feelings ever expressed on earth. And let me say this: If God's feelings and character are like those of Christ, then God is very good indeed. The

---

3   Abba Matta here quotes John 17—one of his favorite passages—in its entirety.
4   John 17:6
5   John 17:20

remark might seem a bit strange in its formulation, but its meaning is extremely profound; and it demonstrates why Christ is God without the shadow of a doubt.

Without Christ, in fact, God would have remained a very big, a very distant and transcendent idea. He would be a great and fearsome being! Who could see Him? Who could know Him or kiss Him? Who could consider himself a close friend or even son of the Godhead? Behold, the fearful God, infinitely removed from our minds, our nature, and our comprehension! In the popular apophatic theology,[6] God is described as the unseen, the unapproachable, the incomprehensible, the uncircumscribed, etc.—just write "un-" followed by the attribute of your choice. But then Christ came and *showed* us (among so many other things) God's *love*. He "disclosed" God to us; we finally knew God, and He became to us very beloved indeed. Christ has given us a picture of God—at once extremely practical and simple—without which He could never really have become an intimate part of our lives.

I could not think of anything to discuss with you tonight except this divine love. For what brought me out here to the monastery in the first place but Christ's ardent love? What caused me to take on the monastic habit and to accept a final severance between myself and the world? This black garment, this new name, this isolated desert, and this calling which is so little understood by the world—nothing could have proffered to me these things but love. Abbas, many pity us and criticize us for leaving the world to stay in the desert; but they do so without right. Christ deigned to leave heaven itself and abide on earth. I have found no other way to fully express my love for God than by this calling. Before, I would express my love for Him through prayer and words, but it did not suffice; I would not find rest and satisfaction in words alone! So I decided to give Him my entire life, and I left the

---

6   Or "negative theology," which attempts to describe God by saying what God is not.

world; and I still give it to Him every day. Of course He rewards me abundantly, but I am not looking for rewards. I seek rather how to renew my love for Him each day. I seek how to offer Him a sincere and unmixed love—not just by external prayers, prostrations, or services—but by a *life* surrendered, even unto death.

Let me speak now of the love Christ placed in our hearts through the Holy Spirit as expressed by St. Paul. Of course you are all familiar with 1 Corinthians 13, so let us read it together.[7] I have told you before, Abbas, that when we speak about love, we speak about the whole of life. Augustine says, "Love, and do what you will."

Once, an abba who was known to be full of love said to me, "I perform my prostrations and pray the psalms in such and such a manner. What is your advice to me?"

I told him, "Those who have gone in the way of love and have experienced that divine mystery are no longer subject to any law. Anything you do, by love, is correct. Whether you spend the whole night in prayer, or prostrations, or singing psalms, it is all good and proper." And why? Because once you have entered into the blaze of divine love, you no longer distinguish between prayer and prostrations, between day and night, between light and dark, between good and bad tidings, between health and sickness. Once love ascends the heart's throne and reigns, life itself becomes a new heaven and new earth.

In truth, Abbas, I cannot fulfill my role as a spiritual father to you except by the way of love. I cannot correct any error in the midst of our gatherings except through love. I cannot increase your spiritual growth even by a hair's breadth except through love. The only thing I have to offer you is love. Remember that the last message Christ delivered to humanity while on earth was love.[8] It is the first and greatest commandment. At the beginning of His preaching, a lawyer

---

7   Abba Matta here reads 1 Cor 12:31—13:13.
8   John 13:34

asked Him about the path to eternal life, and He answered that it was love;[9] and He closed His ministry with the prayer of love to the Father.[10] The message of the Cross itself is founded on love. At the opening of John's Gospel, we are told that God so loved the world that He gave His only Son.[11]

So if a monk builds his life on severe fastidiousness in ritualistic details, timings, and stereotyped prayers—and forgets the work of love—he will be like Abba Isaac when he turns on the generator but forgets to connect it with the electric machinery; and he returns to his cell convinced that all the lights are on, just to have another abba come and tell him the place is all dark. He goes back and finds that he forgot to make a connection. So he does it, the lights turn on, and the joy-filled celebrations begin. So is the monk who strives in asceticism and fasting, who smites his breast and strictly observes his rule of prayer and prostrations, but who knows not how to "trade" in love with his brothers. He has learned not how to love the old and young, the friend and stranger, the guest and laborer, and any other person who crosses his path.

If love ever breaks down in your life, you will be imitating Abba Isaac's disconnected generator. But if your "generator of love" is working properly, all your struggles and prostrations will be converted into a very powerful and mystical energy that will enlighten wondrously; and you will be capable of doing amazing things, even in complete silence. Once love surpasses the level of mere asceticism and fills the heart, then spiritual wealth, and goodness, and blessings in abundance will follow.

That is why, brethren, I repeat so often that our lives are wholly founded on love. Remember the verse, "You shall the love the Lord your God with all your heart, soul, mind, and strength."[12] *Heart, soul,*

9   Luke 10:25
10   John 17
11   John 3:16
12   Matt 22:37; Mark 12:30; Luke 10:27

mind, and strength. I refer to this as the *inner,* unseen divine love. There is also an *outer,* visible divine love. It is indicated by our Lord's saying, "I was hungry, and you fed Me. I was thirsty, and you gave Me drink. I was naked and you clothed Me. I was sick and you visited Me. I was imprisoned and you came to Me . . . for inasmuch as you have done it to the least of My brethren, you have done it to Me."[13] Divine love is practiced on *both* levels: the exterior and the interior; prayer and action. For remember the first command says that you shall love the Lord your God; and the second command is like it, that you shall love your neighbor. The first is the *interior* love, the second the *exterior.* Can anyone love his neighbor and it not show? Never. It will be a very practical and conspicuous love, witnessed by all around, even by unbelievers, who will confess that they are looking upon something very lofty and striking indeed. Love itself serves as a remarkable witness to others. We must become fully devoted disciples of this divine love.

Again, I will say that we *love* on two levels—we are "filled," we are "charged" by heaven, we have our hearts "quickened" by the Holy Spirit—all on two levels. The assurance[14] of the first, inner love is your prayer in secret.[15] Your life with God and love for Him must be carried out *in secret.* No one should be able to catch a glimpse of it. Enter your room, close the door, and take up your place of worship. But do not close the door, then raise your voice for others to hear you; for then you will not have really closed the door, but rather have sounded a trumpet. Every connection that links you with God in divine love must be formed secretly.

The assurance of the second, practical type of love is itself quite

---

13   Parable of the Sheep and Goats; Matt 25:31–44

14   The Arabic phrase Abba Matta employs (*ayit el demun*), which is here rendered *assurance,* indicates the evidence or confirmation that a particular thing exists or is true. It could also be rendered by the words *sign, guarantee, surety, evidence,* or *earnest.*

15   Matt 6:6

surprising. We find it in the Bible: "Do not let your right hand know what your left hand is doing."[16] As I asked you before, can a person really hide a work of love that he does for his neighbor? It's impossible! If a brother is sick, and I run to him with some medicine, who in the monastery won't hear about it? And won't they say, "Wow, did you see how Abba So-and-so went in the middle of the night to help the sick abba? What love!" The publicity, however, will cause me to lose my reward. So what is the assurance that will preserve this act of divine love for me? "Do not let your left hand know what your right hand is doing"—meaning that I might be the one doing the loving act, but I must hide the act, so to speak, from myself. Hiding a loving act from others is often impossible, as when Abba Pishoy runs to and fro throughout the monastery to help Abba Macarius in his need; but a man must hide the good deed *from himself.*

My words might sound curious but not fully understandable. [Let me elaborate.] The "left hand" symbolizes the ambitious self, the ego, the normal human nature that seeks after recognition and honor. The "right hand" symbolizes the work of grace in oneself, or the divine nature that is implanted in the new man, which cannot bear glory for itself but rather for God alone. So, do not let your ego "see" the work of love you perform on your brother's behalf, that you do not get puffed up.

Some of you, abbas, might have tasted this experience. You will do a good work without allowing the slightest whisper within you to suggest that you have done something praiseworthy. At times you might even perform an act of incredible sacrifice, while the brother for whose sake so much love and so much toil is expended appreciates not what you do. He'll say, "Brother, keep helping me; do not leave me!"

And you will say, "I have been with you since 7 AM today, and now it's 6 PM!"

---

16 Matt 6:3

And he will respond, "But remain here."

If your left hand dominates your heart, you might say to him, "That's it! I've been offering my sweat and blood for your sake these many hours, and do you count it a small thing? I'm not helping you anymore." But no, do not let your left hand know what your right hand is doing! Not even until the grave.

[Let us return to the inner love.] I had previously mentioned the verse, "You shall love the Lord your God with all your heart, with all your mind, with all your soul, and with all your strength." Abbas, this is how *prayer* needs to be conducted. Come, let us begin to understand these words, let our minds open up to new meanings, and let us rejoice! But what is prayer? Prayer that is strong, that has purpose, that has meaning, is prayer offered from all the heart, all the mind, all the soul, all the strength. This is the prayer of love. Every prayer offered to God that lacks these four sources—heart, soul, mind, and strength—will result in monotony and dreariness. It is impossible, my brethren, for a person who prays from the fullness of these four springs to be moved by Satan even a bit! Prayer possessed of such singular purpose ascends without any hindrance until it reaches its ultimate destination: the heart of God. I am confident that some of you have tasted this, that when you adopt a sincere posture before God and with childlike simplicity offer up prayer in truth and love, you really feel that the prayer has reached its destination.

I am not placing before you unreasonably high standards. Quite the reverse, I will simplify the practice for you remarkably, even miraculously; and the "miracle" is available to you if you will accept it. Some students once came from De La Salle University and said to me, "Please give us a word."

So I told them, "You have come to a monastery, and here you see me before you as a monk, with a white beard, who has spent many years in monasticism; so it probably seems to you that I am a large figure who has had grand experiences in the spiritual life and an immense knowledge of Christ."

They of course all nodded their heads. So I continued, "Actually, no. Let me tell you who I am and what my life has been.

"When I was a child in the early 1920s, whenever we had a serious problem, my family would stand me up in their midst and tell me, 'Pray.' And I would repeat the Lord's Prayer after them line by line. Then they would recite a prayer of supplication to God regarding the problem, which I would also repeat line by line. We were a poor family and had to send our grain in bags to the bakery to be made into bread. So when the freshly ground grain would arrive at our house from the mill, my parents would use my tiny hand to make the sign of the cross in it before it was sent for baking. To them, the grain felt warm, but to my tender hand it was extremely hot; but I submitted in silence, because we were praying. My inner feelings at that moment were very peculiar. Although I understood very little because I was only four or five years old, the silent presence of my parents and seven siblings about me told me that our circumstances were critical, that the family was facing hardship, but that everything was in God's hands. I was struck by an immense idea of who God is!

"Afterward I completed my education and entered the workforce. But at that point I weighed these things against Scete[17] and found the latter the preferred way—the desert of the saints. So I came here and said to myself, 'Now I am in the company of saints. It is time to experience the spiritual heights!' I immersed myself in prayer, the Bible, and patristic writings, until, little by little, I regained that first childhood experience of God that struck me in the 1920s."

That was the word I gave them. To feel the divine presence; to feel

---

17   Also called Wadi el Natrun, probably the most famous concentration of monastic life in the Egyptian desert, first established for the eremetic lifestyle when St. Macarius of Egypt retired there in the fourth century.

that no barrier exists between myself and God; to feel that a particular issue raised before God is truly heard by Him—*that* is prayer. When I heard my parents say that God was glorified and the hardship ended, I rejoiced. Whenever my family directed me to pray—for prayer was the main role to which I was appointed by my family—I would pray with all my childlike heart. I tell you, brethren, that the act of prayer would absorb my entire being in God's presence. For while praying, all my thoughts and feelings had no object but the prayer, and my mind and focus were totally "used up" in the act. This all would occur although I never did prostrations, or fasted until sundown, or performed any like asceticism. Is this difficult, brethren? If it is feasible for a child, how about for the powers and abilities of a grown man? The only real difficulty is emptying the heart, along with the mind, soul, and strength, of their loads, and devoting them to God and God alone.

Once you achieve this, then takes place that divine connection with God which we call "union." The concept of *union* occupies a very lofty place in Orthodox thought. Union with the Holy Trinity is, indeed, foundational to Orthodoxy. However, it is sometimes misunderstood by certain theologians (who study without spiritual understanding) that union is the end of the road. That is, they teach that *after* we pray a lot, and fast a lot, and spend a very long time in asceticism, *then* will we achieve union with God. No, beloved; union can occur from the age of three or four, if only you are taught to stand and pray before God with all your heart, mind, soul, and strength.

Union with God is accomplished only through love, for "God is love." Love is the only path that can lead to God's heart. Christ consecrated this path by His Blood, for what is Christ's Blood but love? "God so loved the world that He gave His Son's blood."[18] As it is written, "We have confidence to enter the Holy of Holies by the blood of Jesus, by a new and living way which He consecrated for us, that is,

---

18   Paraphrase of John 3:16

His body."[19] This is the path of love that Christ inaugurated by His broken Body and spilled Blood. We enter this path liturgically when we form that splendid circle around the broken Body and shed Blood upon the altar.[20] We walk together in a single line, as it were, upon this new and living way which He consecrated, and enter mystically into God's heart to find *our* place there. And thence we go about our daily work.

So this love that arises through prayer, which I have called the inward or divine aspect of love, is achieved by very simple means. It needs no sophistication. Tell me, do you suppose I was sophisticated at the age of five? Had I any inclination toward asceticism? I tell you with complete sincerity that it took me long periods of struggle to return to that previous childhood state of prayer, to that primitive but immense experience I once had. So, beloved, no one can truly achieve this divine love except *children*. What I tell you is a spiritual law. It is impossible for a person to pray to God with all his heart, soul, mind, and strength unless he become a child at heart.[21]

But the person who makes himself out to be a "big man," with big, important responsibilities, will find all his duties and concerns assail him during prayer. He refuses to be identified as a child and so undergoes the problems of a big man. One thought interrupts his prayer, then another; he repels one thought, and ten more arrive to replace it. Then he comes and complains, "Abba, I am so frustrated; my thoughts won't stop invading my prayer!"

I tell him, "Well, you have made yourself into a big man, so deal with it. But you should say to God, 'Lord, I am Your little child So-and-so. Allow me into Your presence with the face and heart of a child;

---

19 Heb 10:19, 20

20 During Holy Communion in the Coptic Orthodox Church, monks and deacons form a ring around the altar, awaiting their turn to partake of the holy Body and Blood.

21 Matt 18:3

and receive this praise that flows from all my heart, soul, mind, and strength!'"

Ah, the mystery of divine love is consummated in the offering to God of these four "centers," which I have been so often repeating. Heart, soul, mind, strength—but before each one comes the word *all*. Not a bit should remain for yourself. You must approach God *wholly*.[22] And we cannot approach God with all our being except by assuming the simplicity of childhood. Do you see now how the monastic way is based on becoming like children? We need to wake up to love, to wake up to childlikeness, to forget ourselves, to forget our merits, to forget our abilities, and to return to the state of "the youngest in my Father's house."[23]

Whenever I would find myself pressed by hardships or faced with challenging duties, I would go to God and say, "What's going on, Lord? Do You think me greater than I really am? I am just your lowly servant . . ."—and insert my old premonastic name. At that moment I would recall a picture of myself (which I still have) when I was four years old. We tend to forget what we looked like at that young age, so I have purposely preserved the picture for myself. I then say to God, "Look! I am no more than what this picture shows; do not give me more than I can handle. I am a very, very little child!" God would then lift my burdens. But when we all come here and imagine ourselves to be big shots, preachers, fully able men, and have people kiss our hands—oh, the error! You will then stand for prayer and find neither heart nor soul capable of being offered wholly to God.

As the Apostle Paul says, "Seek after the best gifts, but I will show you a better way"[24]—the *way* of divine love. In your practice of the inner, divine love, achieved through prayer, it is Christ who guides

---

22 Abba Matta utters the actual English word in this sentence, apparently with the intention of conveying the double meaning of *wholly* and *holy*.

23 Ps 151:1

24 1 Cor 12:31

your prayer. And whether you're praying with the choir or alone in your cell, He is your second voice. Actually, the truth is that He is not the second voice, but *you* are. "It is not I who live but Christ lives in me."[25] Christ stands transfigured over your entire life, over all your prayer and praise; and the Holy Spirit speaks on your lips. By virtue of the constant and manifold stances of love we make before God, we "put on" the Holy Spirit.

The fathers who were advanced in prayer in divine love were termed *pneumatophoros*—"Spirit-bearer."[26] It seems a daunting title, but I can call you that all the same. I know I can find among you genuine *pneumatophoroi*. The person advanced in prayer with divine love truly puts on the Holy Spirit; and his "clothing" is made evident to all by his conversation, by his countenance, by his eyes, and by his silence.

So the state of inner prayer involves becoming consumed by the Holy Spirit. Christ guides the prayer, but the Holy Spirit crafts the words. Little by little, the Spirit overtakes and subdues the person; the Spirit becomes to him a robe of light. He illumines the heart and also the senses, as Christ said: "If your eye is good, your whole body will be full of *light*."[27] Blessed are those with enlightened eyes, for pure also will be their entire bodies. And how can this occur except by putting on the Holy Spirit? I tell you, only three days of standing before God in sincerity are sufficient to clothe you with the Spirit. Oh, for God's great love!

---

25 Gal 2:20

26 The Arabic translation of the Greek term literally means "those who have put on the Spirit."

27 Matt 6:22, emphasis added

PART II

Christian Living

Called by Christ

1976

Now it happened as they journeyed on the road, that someone said to Him, "Lord, I will follow You wherever You go." And Jesus said to him, "Foxes have holes and birds of the air have nests, but the Son of Man has nowhere to lay His head." Then He said to another, "Follow Me." But he said, "Lord, let me first go and bury my father." Jesus said to him, "Let the dead bury their own dead, but you go and preach the kingdom of God." And another also said, "Lord, I will follow You, but let me first go and bid them farewell who are at my house." But Jesus said to him, "No one, having put his hand to the plow, and looking back, is fit for the kingdom of God." (Luke 9:57–62, NKJV)

This Gospel, my beloved, is about the Christian's calling. The incidents in this chapter all refer to this theme, but in a wonderfully varied way. This is made clear, for example, in the beginning of the chapter, where the Lord appoints the seventy apostles to go and preach.[1] It is important, then, whenever reading Scripture, to note the occasion that introduces a certain discourse—and the occasion here was the Lord's choosing of the seventy for evangelism.

The Pauline reading for today contains these words: "I, therefore, the prisoner of the Lord, beseech you to walk worthy of the *calling* with which you were called,"[2] and a little later on, "and He Himself gave some to be apostles, some prophets, some evangelists, and some pastors and teachers, for the equipping of the saints for the work of ministry, for the edifying of the Body of Christ, till we all come to the unity of the faith and of the knowledge of the Son of God, to a perfect man, to the measure of the stature of the fullness of Christ."[3]

One of the best pictures of what Christ's call entails is found in the reading from Acts for today.[4] It describes Paul's shipwreck and drifting in the sea for a full day and night. His calling involved hardship, *not* comfort. The ship breaks to pieces, he is cast into the sea, he floats to an island, and he is bitten by a serpent. One may ask, what kind of "calling" or "apostleship" is this? To all appearances, Paul was not called by God, but his work was a serious error. According to the incredibly false opinion many hold today, if a person is called by God, he should never undergo sickness or pain, for these would be a sign of God's rejection. But what, then, of Paul? His whole life was replete with suffering.

Let us look at today's Gospel (Luke 9:57–62). It speaks of three young men who approached the Lord with the desire of joining in the ministry of the seventy. And Christ here draws for us a fine distinction between three different types of "callings." Let us see if we ourselves are walking worthy of the calling with which we were called, as Paul exhorts us.

---

1   Luke 9:1–6
2   Eph 4:1
3   Eph 4:11–13
4   Acts 27:1–3

The first man approached Christ with these words: "I will follow You wherever You go." It seems like an offer no one could refuse. Outwardly it makes a very nice and appealing impression on the hearer—but then it quickly brings to mind Peter's assertion too.[5] Peter promised to follow Christ even unto death; but the avowal turned out to be a false one and ended in his triple denial. The problem with this young man's statement is its hastiness. It has a very touching sense of zeal, but the Lord rejoins with an answer that is at once the most concentrated and concise statement recorded in the entire Bible: "The foxes have holes, and the birds of the air have nests, but the Son of Man has nowhere to lay His head."

Christ instantly exposes the falseness of the man's idealistic offer. There are ulterior motives; he wants a share in the *advantages* of service and evangelism. He considered the ministry a means to peace, rest, and mirth; and since a money box was also involved, along with food and shelter, it all seemed very beneficial to him. But the Lord saw straight through the futile and insincere zeal hidden in the request, and perceived instead a lack of preparedness for deprivation and sacrifice. If Christ had not explicitly given His reason, we probably would have questioned why the man was refused. The offer appeared so irresistible! I often encounter similar instances, when people tell me about their walk with God—displaying the same type of zeal as this man, as well as the same hastiness—while their motives are not sound. [6] There is something in their approach that indicates they are coming to relax and take life easy; but such a "calling" is to be rejected.

Christ, nevertheless, from the kindness of His heart, did not refuse him. He did not say, "No, My son, there is no hope for you; return home." He maintained the utmost sensitivity in His words, although the response needed the utmost sternness. He simply said, "Don't

---

5   Matt 26:35
6   Abba Matta refers here to candidates for the monastic life.

you know, son, that foxes have holes to turn into at the end of the day for rest; and birds of the sky have their nests to sleep happily in throughout the whole night; and animals in general live easily and care-free. But if you follow Me, you will experience great difficulties." Here the Lord is putting his mind in the right place; he is correcting the young man's offering of himself.

This disclosure of the man's character reminds me of the parable of the sower. His hastiness corresponds to the seed that fell on the stony ground lacking depth. We may therefore label this personality type the "shallow heart." It seeks a calling but is unsupported by a sturdy heart; it depends rather on appearances. It is just like the seed that was unable to send down any roots into the stony ground; and when the summer wind blew and the heat of the eastern sun beat on the plant, it dried up and died. These are people who hear sermons and receive spiritual counsel with excitement and enthusiasm, but in times of trial they fall. I want to add that *trials* are not limited to hardships; Satan can also submit you to trials of *enticement*, which are often worse. Trials of *adversity* are plainly from the devil, who tries to shake you from the path to the Kingdom of heaven; you are immediately aware of it and resist. (Who won't run from a snake?) But it is more dangerous to be tried by the enticement of prominence and power; in these cases the devil just stays quiet.

He stays quiet because there are lacking the "roots" of grace; the person acts on flawed motives. I have seen this plenty of times in my life in those offering their services to the Church, especially in prospective monks. A man presents himself based on his position and reputation, and with the faulty intention of seeking rest. Then we tell him, "Trials and toil are involved in this," and he says, "Yes, yes, I'm ready for that." He sees before him a pleasant monastery, a comfortable cell, and kind, simple monks who would never bother him; and so *rest* becomes foremost in his mind. So he stays a year or two, until the difficulties arise, and decides to renounce his vows; and all those fleeting hopes he once had fall to the ground. Why? Because he didn't find the rest he desired.

Difficulties will cause a person to closely examine the motives that first brought him to the service or to preaching. And I want to clarify that the call to "Go and preach the Kingdom of God," or the invitation to serve the Kingdom, is not necessarily fulfilled by words. The better way is to announce God's Kingdom by our lives. The life that is devoid of the craving for personal rest leads to success and growth in the service of the Kingdom; and hardships and difficulties only increase its growth. Christ never described the life of ministry as producing rest at the end of the day, or giving one the happy feeling of retiring to a hole like the fox, or letting one sleep contentedly in a nest all night long like the birds. No—it involves tears by night and exhaustion by day. Thus is the Kingdom of God!

Truly, that first young man (of the "shallow heart") is a risky character. He said in effect, "I will follow You wherever You go and will rest wherever You rest; and when You come into the Kingdom, let me sit at Your right hand." When the mother of James and John came to Christ with her request that they sit at His side in the Kingdom, He was extremely displeased and returned a stern refusal. He told them that there was a bitter cup before them to be drunk; and if their eyes were fixed merely on the throne, there would be no hope at all in their services for the Kingdom. Let their minds be riveted instead upon the cup and the cross. "If anyone desires to be My disciple, let him not expect to sit next to Me, nor live comfortably with Me, but to devote his heart to carrying the cross." He also told them, "But you are those who have continued with Me in My trials. And I bestow upon you a kingdom, just as My Father bestowed one upon Me, that you may eat and drink at My table in My Kingdom."[7] Christ Himself will bestow

---

7   Luke 22:28

that favor on them; but they cannot grasp for it themselves. The first young man, therefore, can actually be considered an antagonist to the narrow way. But the hardships we endure for the Kingdom are our boasting and glory!

We now turn to the second man. The interesting thing about him is that he requested nothing himself; he was standing silently by when he found Christ beckoning to him and saying, "Follow Me." He pauses a moment to consider, then responds, "Let me go first"—and this *first* is important—"and bury my father." Christ saw clearly that he was willing to follow Him if he could just go and bury his father; but the Lord also sensed alternative affections playing in his heart. He had a desire to accept the call, but the desire issued from a choked zeal and a stifled ardor. The willingness was there, but there was something else thwarting it—his anxiety and fear of the way. There was a kind of terror in his heart that even prevented him from opening his mouth and saying, "I will follow." He remained silent. But when Christ weighed his heart, He found him worthy of the call. Isn't this astonishing? He found him worthy and so offered, "Follow Me!"

When he said, "Let me go first and bury my father," he actually exposed himself; his problem wasn't obvious, but Christ put His finger directly on it. Why was he afraid? Why was he so hesitant to follow the Lord? Why couldn't he open his mouth to declare his commitment to Christ? The reason is, there was a schism in his heart; and Christ diagnosed it as a fettering to the obligations of the family. His family ties are what caused that inward division and the suffocation of the zeal for the call. The man just stood there silent, confused, alarmed, and divided inwardly; he could not bring himself to say, "I will follow." He didn't even know the reason for his split heart. So Christ attempted to motivate him to cast off the constraints by the invitation to follow.

We may label the second young man's personality type the "divided heart." Half of him sought to do God's work, and the other half was preoccupied with family obligations. Christ saw an "opening" to the man's devotion when He perceived that the half which sought God was a bit stronger than the half bound by flesh and family. So when Christ invited him to follow, and he gave the halfhearted and troubled response about family obligations, He proceeded to administer the bitter medicine. "Jesus said to him, 'Let the dead bury their own dead. But go and preach the Kingdom of God.'"

"Are you yourself dead? Open your eyes! Open your heart! What do you feel?"

"I feel, Lord, that I love You incredibly, more than my own household. And I feel the Spirit moving in my heart."

"Good! That means you are a son of the Spirit, a son of life, a son of the Kingdom. Go!" That is the critical word: *go.*

Let's imagine that the young man said, "I will go!" and followed Christ, and found the chains falling off him.

His family would probably have come to tell him, "You're so late! We've been waiting for you at home."

He would reply, "No, I'm not coming. May God help you in finishing everything, but I have no more to do with it."

"What? What infidelity! What icy and stone-like feelings! This is your own dead father!"

"But I can't anymore."

"What's wrong with him? Something must have happened to him. He doesn't care a thing for his father!"

Then his sister would come wailing, "Are you going to leave me alone!"

"Call your other relatives."

"What about *you?*"

"This is not for me. I have already devoted myself to a higher calling and cannot turn back for any reason at all."

Of course, the father was eventually buried, and they cried and mourned for him as usual. Afterward the discussion of the inheritance would naturally come up, along with the usual infighting; finally they would file lawsuits and hire lawyers on each side until they met in court. But Christ offered him the better counsel: "as for you, go and preach the Kingdom." O you who have received the call, and have let a cloud overshadow it, throw off those constraints of the flesh, and go forth! Proclaim the Kingdom of God.

This second type actually appeals strongly to my affections, and I like him very much. I personally was not so during my early life; I was never restrained by the duties of the family. However, I sympathize strongly with those who are of such a disposition. It is a very natural and human nature; it is beautiful in its humanity, and I could never disdain it. But I become intensely disturbed when this type acts as an obstruction to the Kingdom of heaven. It is good, my friend, to fulfill your responsibilities toward your family. It is very good indeed to attend to the needs of your home, your lonely mother, your sister, and your father who is near death. I could never object to these things. *However*, if you sense in your heart the Spirit moving, and eternal life calling, go forth immediately. If no one is found to do the burying, then even the angel Raphael—from the book of Tobit, which speaks of many deaths and burials—will descend and get the job done. The dead will get buried. "But as for you, go and preach the Kingdom of God."

Go and proclaim that *light* that has dawned in your heart! Proclaim that *life* that has taken up its abode within you! And if you sense the Spirit moving inside you, be extremely careful lest you divide the inspiration in two: half for God and half for obligations. You never can! For the obligations will assert themselves and overwhelm you; and you will be continually attending to this or that duty until you're sixty or seventy. Your mother dies and leaves behind your uncle. Your uncle dies and leaves behind your niece. Your niece is not married and lives alone, poor thing! You jump from relative to relative until a similar restraint is also placed on you by neighbors. And the whole time you are sacrificing the cause of the Kingdom for the sake of cares and duties.

I will never forget a man I once knew who was worthy of the priesthood, and so I called him.[8] I said, "Will you come be a priest?" He asked where exactly, and I replied, "In such-and-such a church."

I offered him the ministry of a small church as a test, because I knew he had his eye on a large and prominent one. He responded, "No, I won't be able to, because I have a certain career which will go awry if I leave." He actually desired to be placed in the large church, and, in fact, that would have been his future place of service. The hindrance was not a friend or family member needing burial, but a career. And thus will human emotion quench the call to service if a person gives preference to earthly duties over the call of God.

There is another reason the Lord answered the young man as he did when he asked to go bury his father. The man was a rather shrewd and clever person, and he wanted to stump Christ by putting Him in an awkward position. His words implied, "Don't You know the commandment that says 'Honor your father and mother'? You've asked me to follow, but my father is sick and on the verge of death. Let me go and stay the last few days with him, and bury him; then I will return."

Christ's response was strong but in a hidden way. "Let the dead bury their own dead: let those living in this world worry about the cares of this world. But I am calling you to the Kingdom."

---

8   During a short period in the early days of his monastic life, Abba Matta was appointed as the episcopal "steward" or deputy for the city of Alexandria, which involved performing certain ecclesiastical functions usually executed by a formal bishop. Since the bishop of Alexandria bore the historical title of patriarch of the See of Alexandria, but for practical reasons had to reside in Cairo, the steward was charged with the supervision of the Alexandrian churches in his place. One of the steward's roles was to nominate eligible men for ordination at the hands of the patriarch.

Here the Lawgiver is claiming precedence over the Law. It is the Law's command versus the Lawgiver's command: "*I say to you, 'Come,'* and do you refer back to the *law?*" If a person hears the Spirit or Christ calling in his heart, he is no longer under the law.[9] We can even consider it a mini-doctrine that the Lawgiver reserves the right to supersede the Law. The Lawgiver, in fact, always calls us to what is *higher* than the Law.

We come now to the third man. "Lord, I will follow You, but let me first go and bid them farewell who are at my house." This *first* is a very, very strange condition. Why do you add it if you've promised to follow? Is it that, having become a follower, you still have authority over yourself? "Let me go first and bid farewell." The request looks at first perfectly fitting. Is there any problem with it? But how many times have I personally fallen for this trick! A candidate will come to me and ask, "Abba, would you just permit me to stay at home a short while for my mother's sake? My father also is old and weak. And my siblings too need my help."

Then I, in my naïveté, am dragged by my human emotions and grant him his request. "Fine. Go, say your last goodbyes to your mother and family." But ah, not one was able to say a last goodbye to his mother and peel himself away from her bosom again! That last goodbye will remain fastened to your mind even until your beard greys. But if you were able to leave the world without a last parting greeting to anyone, then the call of Christ will be able to gain you even while in the world. And every time the world comes to mind, you will remember your severance from it, as though by the clean cut of a knife.

Woe to the man who offers those last goodbyes to his father and mother! They will remain stuck like an odor to his clothes and to his mind at all times. He who returns to say goodbye to his family does not actually say goodbye to them but to the Kingdom. He can no

---

9   Gal 5:18

longer enter the Kingdom with the same intensity of zeal and power. And if he goes out to serve while still conscious of an attachment to his family, it becomes a hundred times harder to sever them than if he had done so while he was in the world. It requires a heavy knife to cut the emotional ties that bind a person if already on the road; but if he cuts them while still near his family, the issue is sealed. If the heart must choose between family and God, and it chooses God in the family's presence, then not only will the man be certain of the decision, but the family will too. However, if the last goodbyes and kisses are indulged in, there is no hope; the devil will pester you for the rest of your life with the whisper, "Mama, Mama!"

I want to give you an example from the Old Testament.[10] Remember when Elijah went to the widow in Zarephath and asked for something to eat, and she responded, "Oh, all I have is a handful of flour and a bit of oil. I'm going to just make them into a cake that my son and I might eat once more and die."

He said, "Okay, but make me a cake *first*."

What a stiff heart! Here's a poor woman dying of starvation, and her son is stuck to her bosom, and you, a big old prophet, want to eat as the poor kid stares at you? "Yes." Why, O Elijah? "Because I will eat it in the name of the Lord. Maybe God will have compassion as I eat and grant His grace." And grace was given: the flour and oil never ran out until the famine expired.

God comes first, then body; God first, then food; God first, then clothes; God first, before any earthly thing! But to say, "Let me go first and greet my family," will never work. Once you've placed God second in your life, He can never be first in anything at all!

In truth, although this young man was seemingly the most easy-going of the three, the Lord was the sternest with him. It would take only a half-hour to go bid farewell to his family, but he turned out the

---

10   1 Kin 17:8–15

most risky prospect—because he was the most subject to his emotions. He was his mother's little boy; although he was a grown man, the umbilical cord was still intact. He was tied to his mother, tied to the family, tied to the neighborhood, tied to the friends, tied to the country, tied to his life. This is one of the most troublesome personality types when it comes to obeying the call. Its possessor is extremely weak. His eyes are riveted on the past. The smallest hardship or the slightest rebuke makes him shudder. He constantly thinks of forsaking the call and going back. To put it bluntly, he is not a man.

So the first man we designated as the "shallow heart" and the second as the "divided heart." The third man represents the "fragile heart." His heart is infantile; he remains childish his entire life. I can't really call him a *child* because we are all children of God. But the smallest thing can upset him and push him to tears. His fault requires surgical intervention: he needs the Holy Spirit to cut off the emotional chains. And we see now why Christ's response to him was the most austere of the three.

You've all seen, beloved, a man plowing the ground.[11] He pulls the plow from behind, while the sharp iron cuts the ground, but his eyes are always before him. What is he focused on? The guiding line! The line indicates his path, and he follows it perfectly. If he looks back for a moment, he goes off track. He will either veer right and ruin the previous plow lines or veer left and ruin the pattern. At that point it's almost impossible to fix; all the subsequent plow lines become skewed, and the whole work is bungled up. The error can extend to even a hundred acres. And the interesting thing is that the oxen—which symbolize the mind and conscience—will follow the previous plow lines because they are so well trained to exactly follow the previous plow lines. It is an amazing sight. They will follow a remarkably straight

---

11 Farming was one of the many disciplines in which the monks of Abba Matta's monastery excelled.

course if the line is right. Christ really did use the perfect analogy. "If you put your hand on the plow and look back, you cannot follow Me." Beware, brethren! Be very wary of looking back!

I want to conclude my remarks on this Gospel passage with my heart's desire for you all. I pray that God raise us above the flesh to be worthy of the call. I pray that we look not for worldly rest, nor fear worldly threats, nor be lured by earthly enticements. Let us judge ourselves lest we be judged! I fear, beloved, lest after this long life we hear, "Depart from Me, I do not know you."[12] I fear lest our lives be a futile path! From this day and this hour, let us entreat God earnestly to grant us the spirit of judgment that we might judge ourselves. And I continually entreat God to grant us attentive hearts, even if it requires the sharp knife of grace to cut off every constraint that binds us to the flesh and the world. Let us set our faces upon the Kingdom of God and have the goal clearly before our eyes, that by our tears we might wash away the defilement of sin, and that God might renew His covenant with us every morning.

---

12 Matt 7:23

Peace in the Christian Home

1975

Hear the words of the Gospel: "Whatever house you enter, first say, 'Peace to this house.' And if a son of peace is there, your peace will rest on it; if not, it will return to you."[1] Our discussion this morning will be on the words, *Peace to this house.* The Christian "home" indicates the family: father, mother, and children. When the Lord charged the disciples to grant peace to a house, He did not mean a mere oral expression of peace. Christ's word always carries with it power and an energizing authority. So when an apostle, priest, or servant says, "Peace to this house," he is really granting peace. And when Christ said to the sinful woman, "Go in peace,"[2] His words really infused an empowering peace into her from within. So the peace which is given to the Christian home is a *gift.*

What is *peace?* "Peace" has become a cheap slogan these days, and it's used all day in the streets for trivial greetings; but the actual

---

1   Luke 10:5, 6
2   Luke 7:50

word possesses the highest spiritual and theological significance. It is enough for me to say that Christ was given the title *King of Peace*; and the Gospel itself is called the *Gospel of Peace*. We must pay very close attention to the word's meaning, for we are all incredibly lacking in this virtue, as every tongue will confess. The world for the most part is deprived of peace, and nearly every home is devoid of the peace spoken of by Christ. Why?

Peace is an inner state of the heart and of the mind. But Christian peace is not a mere psychological condition; rather, it's a *relationship*. Christian peace flows from the believer's relationship with God and with other people. It's impossible for a person to have a good, peaceful relationship with God and not enjoy peace with others. So if our relationship with God or others suffers, our peace will flee from us. Every person who does not feel a full, deep, eternal peace within him will find his relationship with God distorted. There is a hard verse, which I am reluctant to quote, but here it is: "There is no peace for the wicked."[3] Any deformation in our relationship with God, or friends, or family, or colleagues, or even with enemies, causes our peace to flee. That is why Christ focused strongly on man's relationship with his neighbor. Why else did He say, "Love . . . love . . . love . . ." even to the point of loving our enemies? Because He desires peace to sink deep within us; for without this, He cannot reign over our hearts. A person cannot be called a "son of the Kingdom" if he has not experienced this rest and confidence of heart.

Another one of the important traits of Christian peace, my beloved, is that it is *lasting*. If your peace is ever cut off one day, that means the King of Peace is not reigning over your heart. No circumstances can steal a Christian's peace as long as it is Christ ruling over his will, conscience, and mind. So what makes peace lasting? It is so when it is not based upon external conditions and does not move with changing

---

3   Is 57:21

circumstances. This peace remains the same in tribulation as in ease, in disease as in health, in poverty as in wealth. So we can consider this the central and foundational attribute of Christ's peace: that it endures.

Lasting peace does not arise from the earth but comes down from heaven; it transcends the material realm and all its business; it encompasses all of a person's circumstances and activities; and it is a peace which connects a person with eternal life. Blessed is the man who receives his peace from heaven! He can never be shaken, because he has bound his life, his beginning and end, to heaven. Earth no more has authority over him; external events no longer possess the ability to shake him. Blessed is the man who has become a citizen of heaven! Does this mean he lives on earth without a nationality? He who is a citizen of heaven also becomes a citizen of earth of the highest degree. The person who lives with God becomes an excellent countryman of earth, because he executes his earthly duties with the utmost faithfulness. Why? Because the peace and confidence in his heart make him a solid man.

Do you know what the opposite of peace is?—Turbulence of heart and mind. The person who has a turbulent heart and mind cannot execute his duties well, neither at home nor elsewhere. So we begin to understand the profound meaning of "Peace to this house"; it is a gift from Christ, and the first gift granted to a house by the messenger of God. God's messenger enters a home, and without even speaking, his presence radiates peace; for he is himself, of course, full of peace. If a person lacks calmness and serenity of heart, how will he offer it to others? So the priest or servant who lives in God's peace will radiate it to others, as a gift, and as a power which energizes the entire house. The occupants will remark, "We don't understand how, once this person entered the house, peace descended on our home!" It's a mistake to think this a blessing of the servant. It's the very power of Christ, a heavenly blessing which always attends God's herald.

When the angels rejoiced on the day of the birth of Christ, the King of Peace, they said, "Glory to God in the highest," then what?— "Peace on earth, and to men of goodwill," which is the most accurate translation. Note very well the joining of the two expressions: "Glory to God in the highest" and "Peace on earth." It's as if to say that, through Christ's birth, the eternal glory of heaven was transformed into eternal peace on earth. As long as glory is to be found in heaven, so long will peace be found on earth—until the end of days, among men of goodwill.

And why? Because Christ came down to earth. As we read, "I saw Satan fall like lightning."[4] Satan no more wields authority after Christ's incarnation; and the King of Peace has established His rule over the Church, over God's people, and over every family. So when the priest carries God's peace in his heart and life, and grants it to the Christian family, he gives a very great gift indeed! He is enthroning Christ as King over the home and over the hearts. And when Christ's peace reigns over the family, every trouble has an escape, every disease has consolation, and every poverty has contentment; the inward life is elevated above all pain and strife.

My beloved, those who live in Christ have their peace renewed day by day. This is a *gift*, the immensity of which I'm laboring to communicate to you! Those who live in Christ do not simply receive a one-time advantage from God, then live the rest of their lives off it; rather, His gifts are renewed for us every day. There is a verse I've loved my entire life: "Your mercies are new every morning, O God of Jacob."[5] God's peace is renewed in the Christian's heart *all the time*, and especially at times of changing circumstances. Every situation has its peace. And if the Christian is attentive—and I wish that every Christian would live in a state of inner attentiveness of

---

4   Luke 10:18
5   See Lam 3:22–24.

heart—he will find that every situation he faces has its own peace.

The person who is not practiced in the life with God will complain, "I pray and read the Bible; but when I engage in the world's business, my peace vanishes because of the problems encountered from colleagues and acquaintances, and even from traffic. I go home with my peace completely gone." No, no—this is a trivial peace, one which changes with changing circumstances. It is not from God, not Christ's peace, not from heaven, not from the King of Peace!

There's another beautiful verse that I desire, O Lord, that everyone memorize: "The Lord is with you while you are with Him. If you seek Him, He will be found by you; but if you forsake Him, He will forsake you."[6] I deem this verse to encompass all of theology, all of the Bible, and all of our life with God. This is a promise, my beloved! Every verse is a promise from the Spirit. Take it as a fixed law. Beloved, why do you all respect the laws of earth so much but not the laws of heaven? I marvel.

Any person, for example, is afraid to jump from a height of three meters. If I say, "Jump!" he says, "No, I'll fall and break my arm!"

"What are you afraid of?" I respond, and he says, "The law of gravity." So you hold the law of gravity in such high esteem, but lightly esteem the laws of the Kingdom of heaven? Believe me, and I say this with the utmost certainty from my reading and experience and counsel—that the laws of the Spirit, and of the Kingdom, and of the Bible, are stronger and more fixed than all the physical laws of earth. So take each verse as a certainty. No physical law indeed can be overturned except by a heavenly law, as when our Lord walked on water. For by walking on the water, as well as by His Ascension, He was showing us that His authority and divinity were derived from a source higher than earth.

Not only are spiritual laws stronger than physical laws, not only should you respect spiritual laws as much as physical laws, but I wish

---

6   2 Chr 15:2

to lead you higher. You ought to respect spiritual laws *more* than the physical; trust any verse you encounter more than even the established theories of science. A person will tell you, "This is a proven scientific theorem, depend on it." Well then, how is it we so trust in the laws of changing matter but little regard the unchanging things of the Spirit? They once said that the atom could not be split; and the student who would claim on a test that it could be split would fail. Today, a student is failed if he says that the atom *cannot* be split. These scientific laws were taught us *ipso facto*; but today they have split not only the atom but everything within the atom too. So you see how physical laws and theoretical ideas are changing, and sometimes completely reversed, whereas the laws of the Kingdom of heaven are unchanging and unalterable. The truths of heaven are fixed; the verses of the Bible are powerful and can never be erased or repealed; neither man nor circumstances can ever resist them.

Consider this: "Seek and you will find." This is a *law*, my beloved. A person can never seek and not find. I believe you all understand now what I mean by a *spiritual law*. "Ask and you will receive." It is impossible, impossible I say, for a person to stand before God, regardless of who he is, regardless of how bad his sinful life is, and not receive. The adulterous woman stood before Christ, even without her assent, and they assailed her viciously; but she stood before Him and received grace and salvation. Simply by entering God's presence does a person receive glory! "Ask and you will receive." The woman stood in all her sinfulness, and Christ had compassion. *Compassion* is one of Christ's greatest traits, one which I would like to impress upon your hearts; He is extremely tender and kind. The elders and Pharisees said, "She ought to be stoned by Moses' law. What do *You* say?" He looked at them and pierced their hearts and consciences, and they were all convicted; for he who willfully holds fast to his sins cannot stand in the Lord's presence. He flees, he runs, for darkness cannot face light. The poor woman felt her sin; it's truly enough for a person to realize his sin. To simply feel oneself a sinner immediately renders a person worthy to enter the Lord's presence and to receive His power, forgiveness, and purification.

"Has anyone condemned you?"

"No, Lord."

"Neither do I condemn you; go *in peace*."

Beloved, why isn't the Christian house filled with peace? My heart is torn apart at the bitter things I hear happening in homes—things that evoke tears! Families are divided and weary. There is no peace between father and children; between mother and children; between husband and wife; or between siblings. Why, oh why, is peace lacking? I said before it's a divine promise; and it's also a heavenly injunction. This injunction is a single phrase that was declared by angels' voices, and written into Scripture by the Spirit, and comforts us until today: "Peace on earth, and to men of goodwill."

So why is there no peace in the Christian family? Oh, my brethren, the reason is clearly perceived in this verse: "My peace I leave with you. My peace I give unto you—not as the world gives."[7] Here, brethren, is the secret to our afflictions and schisms, and to every family's weariness: the Christian family today seeks the peace given by the world. Listen closely. There are only two alternatives: either we seek the world's peace and so miss Christ's peace; or we seek Christ's peace, and the world's peace gets "added in" for us.

Christ's peace subdues all adversity in life; it makes heat into coolness and rest, desert into paradise, and enemies into peacemakers. Once you are reconciled to Christ, you will find the brother with whom you have been at odds knocking on your door. This happened recently with a family present with us, which suffered from a fifteen- or twenty-year-old division. I sat with the instigator of the problem

---

7 John 14:27

and told him, "My friend, right yourself; life is short and our days few. You have to renew your relationship with Christ, or you won't be able to meet Him after death."

His heart was moved, a thing I love to see, and he said, "All right, I will reconcile with my brother." He met with his brother, and they found that the factors causing the division were immediately resolved.

Brethren, I speak to you with the utmost certainty, for I speak to you by the laws of the spirit, which exert their power over all physical laws. Believe me when I say that if a person ever meets with antagonism from a hard situation, or from a difficult life, or from family, brother, father, mother, work, enemy, or even government—if he stands rightly before God and reconciles with Him in his heart, all such antagonism and strife will vanish in a moment. And he will find the way before him full of peace.

Brethren, listen well to what I say: if we seek the world's peace, we will not taste God's peace. We might enjoy the world's peace for a season—I don't deny that money in the bank allows us to travel to Europe, to buy whatever we want, to wear the best clothes—but that's it. It also spoils children; a man with two hundred thousand pounds in the bank might find his daughter led astray by the wealth, and he will say, "I am willing to give away all my money if only my daughter would return to me." When we request the world's peace, we will have to pay a price. But what is that price? Losing God's peace. And not only that, but even the world's peace we will have to "pay"—that is, we will lose. Bitter tears will flow, the heart will be wounded, and what is our gain? Why do we continue to walk with our eyes shut until we fall into the pit? Why don't we open our eyes? Open your spiritual eyes!

Running after the world's peace brings satisfaction for only a fleeting moment. We will eat the best food, enjoy good health, go on luxurious trips to see delightful sights, and come back to tell our stories to our poor friends and sadden their hearts. Truly, we sadden a poor family's hearts when we sit and describe to them our enviable world travels—but it's all false, a false trip, a false joy!

I once knew a gloomy and depressed man whose doctors told him to go abroad and visit the world in order to eliminate his depression, since every medication he took failed to help. He saw the world and benefited nothing, so he eventually came to speak with me. He said, "I've spent several thousand pounds going on trips, but my soul is still heavy and tired; please help me."

I told him, "You see, the world's peace doesn't bring inner peace; let me show you the way."

Brethren, let me tell you frankly, ninety-nine percent of poor homes live in peace, and ninety-nine percent of wealthy homes live without peace. I am telling you actual statistics. But the poor home that desires money and wealth is also devoid of peace. And likewise the wealthy home, if it is free of covetousness, and would be content to live as the poor, and even does so, and rejoices in giving—lives in peace.

Money, my brethren, is a very troubling and bothersome thing. Imagine with me a man walking to the bank with ten thousand pounds in his pocket, and a friend meets him along the way and invites him to coffee at the local café. He nervously refuses and says, "I can't, I'm . . . I'm . . . busy." He needs to get the money to the bank and is scared to death of losing it. And if the money is at home, he loses sleep. He gets new bolts for the doors and the best doorman but still can't sleep. He puts it into the bank but worries that the bank will go bankrupt. A bank can disappear in a moment, as well as any insurance policy. My beloved, money can never comfort the heart of man or bring him peace—it's a great lie!

And what is there besides money? Power? Weapons? But the more powerful a man is, the more prone is he to fighting and war. The more weapons he owns at home, the more restless is his heart. A man who owns a gun is always on the brink of a fight. But the man who owns no gun, not even a stick, has this—"Peace to this house." Neither physical power nor weapons can ever offer peace and rest.

And what else steals our peace? Desires of the flesh? Beloved, this point is obvious and does not need much talk. Any violation of God's law, especially in the area of purity and bodily cleanliness, exacts a heavy price in bitterness of conscience for the rest of one's life. A sin of the flesh remains revolving in a person's mind even though he become a saint. It plays in the mind and breaks the heart. What does a man gain? Even if he enjoys himself all day for twenty-five years of his youth, at a point it all ends; then manhood comes, followed by old age, bringing with it a withered body and a wasted conscience, until he enters the grave without hope. *Unless* he stands before Christ to be washed in His Blood and to receive strength.

Beloved, I have never seen a young boy or girl give themselves the liberty to live in sin, who did not pay for it later in difficult relations with their spouse and kids in older life. God's law cannot be voided. It is *impossible*, I say, and I tell you in Christ's name and by the strength of biblical law that it is impossible to violate God's law of purity and not pay the price. So what will we gain from the pleasures of the flesh? *Bitterness*, my beloved. I don't like to talk much about this issue, but I was compelled because one of the greatest causes for our loss of peace is violation of the law of purity. And if there weren't a greater and stronger principle helping man, called the law of repentance, there would be no hope for man.

Let me give you an illustration. If I throw a nail into the canal, it will sink to the bottom. But if I tie the nail to a piece of wood (I'm thinking of the wood of the Cross), and attach them both to a crimson thread (you understand the meaning), and throw the nail in, it will float on the water's surface. What happened to the law of gravity? It wasn't cancelled but instead overcome, "defeated," by the law of floating bodies. Man likewise is ever borne up over every depth by the Spirit, who is our crimson thread that ties us to the Body and Blood of Christ. But if the thread isn't tight, the nail will sink; and then Christ's Body will not benefit me. The nail is tied to the wood—I am united to Christ's Body—but if the line is made limp, the nail sinks. This means the Spirit is not working in me. I might be baptized and take communion, but the thread is limp. How do we make the thread tight? By fasting, by vigils, by prayer, by true and faithful worship. When we do this, the Spirit is made active within, the thread is tightened, and the law of sin is overcome. "The law of the Spirit in Christ Jesus has made me free from the law of sin and death."[8] There are *two laws*, and both possess incredible power. But Christ be thanked, "There is therefore now no condemnation to those who are in Christ Jesus, who do not walk according to the flesh, but according to the Spirit."[9]

Our good God, O Lord of every family, Father of all orphans and widows and every struggling soul, Father of the entire Church and her Bridegroom, grant peace to Your house and Your people, to every family and every individual. O Son of God, and King of Peace . . . *Epouro ente tihrini, moi nan entek hirini.*[10] May Your peace dwell in our hearts, so that all people may return to You and You to them; that they may live with You and You with them; that they might receive Your good and heavenly things; that they might not turn to the right or left, nor request help from man, but rely on You and behold Your power and victory; that their tongues might praise You all their days! O King of Peace, rest Your peace today on Your people and Your Church, that they might rejoice in the eternal life which You give them. Reign, O King of Peace, reign over our homes, that we might rejoice in You forever. Amen.

---

8   Rom 8:2
9   Rom 8:1
10   The opening line of one of the most famous Coptic hymns: "O King of Peace, grant us Your peace."

A Word to Married Couples

1975

I wish for you to know that the mystery[1] into which you entered on your wedding day is an eternal gift. It is given as a source of power—that is, it grants the husband and wife strength to live righteously both inside *and* outside the home. For this holy mystery effects a very high and spiritual type of "circumcision" for the heart, for the eyes, and for all the senses; it is a mystery that preserves both husband and wife in the purity of Christ.

You also should understand that it is a union which continues into heaven. That is why Christ forbade divorce; do not be deceived: divorce is a lie! The bond that links the spouses is spiritual and eternal. It is like the sacrament of chrismation that follows baptism. Let me clarify with an image. Imagine an angel coming down from heaven and stamping the newly baptized soul with a seal of light. From that moment, it is a soul registered in heaven; and every angel, as well as

---

1   The word may also be translated "sacrament," and so throughout the discourse.

every devil, who sees the seal knows it belongs to a child of God. But say that such a soul rejects Christ, renounces God, and abandons the faith—what happens to the seal? It can never be erased! On earth, such a person would perhaps cause grief among family; but in heaven, where the seal is visible to all, the act of apostasy is witnessed by tens of thousands.

So marriage is a spiritual, luminous act that seals every member of the body and destines it for the purity of Christ. It furthermore makes husband and wife one body, that they might come into one inheritance in heaven. They can never again be separated. Sometimes one spouse will say, "I'm not speaking to you; we're at odds right now!" or simply give the other the silent treatment without any explanation. How senseless! Can the right hand be divided from the left? Can the right eye separate itself from the left? Impossible. The spouses are eternally joined; they are one indivisible body. So every time an offense is committed between the spouses, they must remember that the nuptial mystery preserves the oneness of spirit; it provides a state of perpetual reconciliation and peace. It's as if Christ has the husband in one hand and the wife in the other, as they walk together, and the husband tells the wife, "I'm not speaking to you." Could he do that? Remember who it was who said, "What God has joined together let not man separate."[2] We often disregard and disrespect the words of Christ. Whatever God has brought together not even Satan can separate! How can a marital rift occur in the presence of the risen Christ?

But why do divisions arise? Why does discord occur? It is because each spouse's ego wants its own concerns to be always recognized. "But Abba," you will say, "we come from very dissimilar families, and we live by different principles and opinions. How can you say we will be *one*?"

I will tell you. Once a person gives up his own "self," at that moment he obtains Christ's "self." Oh, what peace and joy result when both

---

2   Mark 10:9

husband and wife give up their respective "selves"! Laughter then fills the house, and all things become good and wonderful. Even wrongs and apologies flow easily and good-naturedly between the spouses. Then the will to reconcile and forgive comes *before* the need to admit wrong and apologize. And Christ, who is present among them, at every moment does the work of unity.

We may also compare the sacrament of marriage to the sacrament of baptism. Why is it that a person can repent at any moment, even to the very last moment of life? It is because the blessings that he received with the new birth are always available to him. In marriage, likewise, you are always immersed in Christ. Each time you stand to pray together, Christ comes to bless you and to confirm and fortify the mystery that was completed between you. If I may express it thus, the two of you "get married" every single day. Do you remember how happy you were the day of your wedding? Do you remember how your hearts thumped with joy as you stood in church listening to the prayers? This is how it always ought to be! You must be "remarried" every day in God's hands. This mystery must be developed and consummated to the point that it changes your whole thinking process. I do not deny that we all have different personalities and viewpoints, but how great it is when each spouse submits to the mind of Christ![3]

There is another reflection which I always like to share when I am speaking to married couples. One of the mystery's most splendid characteristics is the fact that the husband complements his wife's weaknesses, while the wife complements the weaknesses of her husband. Once Christ has brought you both together, all of the husband's faults are yours, O wife, and all the wife's faults are yours, O husband. So the husband can no longer count up the wife's faults against her, nor can the wife count up the husband's. If they do, they've

---

3   2 Cor 2:16

fallen outside the bounds of the mystery. This is a rule in theory; but how do we apply it in practice?

Let me give you an illustration. Say a young boy gets sick. The father comes and asks what is wrong.

"My stomach hurts, Daddy."

"Your stomach, my son?" the dad responds. "Oh, if it were only my stomach instead of yours!" And then the father stands before God and entreats Him for the son's recovery, even if it would require that the father adopt his son's pain.

And the mother too: "Lord, my child is so ill and weak! Take the pain away from him and place it *on me*; I am willing to endure it!" These words I used to hear from my own mother. She would enter her room alone to pray, but I could still hear her: "Lord, take away all illness from my children and place it in my own blood!"[4] And her words still ring in my ears until today: *My own blood, O Lord.*

So what I wish to tell you before God is that the day you accepted each other in marriage, you also accepted each other's flaws. The considerate wife will say to her husband, for example, "Forgive me, my husband, and please bear with me. You see, I get irritated so easily, and I have a quick temper, and I raise my voice inadvertently."

And the kind husband will respond, "Oh, but you don't know how much I'm praying for you already! Why are you so upset? Do not be distressed. If only I could bear your troubles instead of you! Just tell me how to help you. I wish never to see you so sad and disturbed."

Hearing such words will fill her with happiness; and she may well weep for joy, and weep that God has given her such a husband who lifts her troubles, along with her gloom and anxieties—but most of all, who lifts her errors.

And the husband will say to her, "My wife, I have so many defects about me; please be patient with me."

---

4   A metaphorical Eastern expression.

And she will respond, "Oh, there is no one like you! I love you with all my heart, and you are the greatest person in my life." Once he hears these words, his flaws get smaller and smaller until they vanish away.

Such is Christianity, and such is the mystery of marriage! If only this attitude were adopted, the adversary would never be able to invade the couple's union! Reconciliation, comfort, peace, and happiness would fill all their days. But, alas, the inconsiderate wife tells her husband, "I will never, never forget how one month after our wedding you said to me such and such!" And similar comments are made after twenty or thirty years have passed. But if we hold grudges and wrongs against each other to this extent, when will peace ever come? How will joy ever arise?

And then there is the question of salvation: how will you receive together your eternal inheritance? Or is marriage just for this earth? Indeed, it plays an enormous role in the salvation of the spouses, as well as the salvation of the children and of the grandchildren. Yes, you must know that a great responsibility was placed upon you the day you accepted each other! You took a vow before the Church and the angels declaring that you are now responsible for the salvation of your spouse and of your offspring.

But how is it that we still judge each other in the face of Christ's words: "If you forgive others their trespasses, your trespasses will also be forgiven"?[5] He spoke these words in a very direct, childlike spirit; but we have hard heads, and we don't want to believe Him. He even said it in the "Our Father." If we forgive others, we will be forgiven; if we refuse to forgive others, our sin will remain. Does the command need any further explanation? In the day you refuse to forgive your wife or husband, all blessing and communion will vanish, and you will never feel peace or grace. Your sin will be bound to you! But when you forgive each other, love will reign. And when love reigns, it means God is reigning.

---

5   Matt 6:14

When I was the director of the people's council[6] in Alexandria, we mediated 105 divorce cases which, in the name of Christ, were all successfully resolved. But they were all based on trivialities! Are there really any trivial flaws that can justify splitting up a marriage? With God as my witness, there are none. They are rather illusions and falsehoods which Satan uses to divide and distance the married hearts. Could there ever really be a good reason for the husband to devastate his wife? Can the wife ever be justified in turning her back on her husband when he returns home, going in her room, and shutting the door? These are crimes against God's love!

But how wonderful is it when, for example, the wife falls ill, and the husband takes a day off work to stay with her. In that day she will identify her husband with her heart. Again, the husband might come home one day, loathing himself as he rings the doorbell; but then the wife opens, takes him in her embrace, and kisses him. And, by the way, this is a very necessary habit, which if it is lacking, you are both remiss. The husband should never meet his wife at the door without kissing her. Why aren't you all living this way? Why is your love fragmented?

Strive to be good stewards of the nuptial mystery. If you are faithful, you will find this blessed mystery grow and fill up your lives, and you will sense very strong ties developing between the both of you. Marriage, like all the mysteries, is full of *power*. But the continuance of the power depends on an intimate proximity to Christ; for without Him, a bitter turmoil will engulf you.

I speak these words to all married couples in the lands of immigration; your estrangement in foreign lands demands an even closer dependence upon God's Word, for it contains those precious promises and commands by which we may overcome the world. Without His word, we cannot live. Without His word, marriage

---

6   A governing body in the Coptic Church composed entirely of laymen, in which Abba Matta played a prominent role before his monastic life.

becomes a burden, a trial, and an anxiety. This is what causes people to utter, "I wish I never got married." Also, as parents in immigrant lands, you carry a tremendous responsibility; for who will comfort and guide your children but you? But when you yourselves do not live in joy or peace, what can you pass on to your kids except an anxious mind? But I have hope in Christ Jesus that you will heed these words. And know that the holy mystery which you received is an asset greater than any career or any fortune you could ever amass. It is a unique investment which is given especially to you, upon which you may draw and which you may enjoy the rest of your life.

PART III

On Scripture

The Temptation of Our Lord

FIRST SUNDAY IN GREAT LENT, 1973

You know, brethren, that we are in one of the most important seasons of the Church. You just heard how the Lord entered the desert by the Spirit to be tempted forty days and forty nights ... and He was alone. We know why Christ was baptized in the Jordan, why He offered Himself up on the Cross, and why He rose from the dead. And before us now is one of those works of our Lord which is greatly honored and celebrated by the Church—for fifty-five days the Church revels in it by her hymns, sermons, and constant activities. After being baptized, He went out alone into the wilderness, fasting for forty days and forty nights. What did the Lord do in this period, and why did He do it? In truth, the work Christ accomplished in the wilderness, from the Church's standpoint, was a *collective* work. And from your and my standpoint, it was a *personal* work.

Of course you are all Bible readers, or else you wouldn't have left the Egyptian city to come and pray in the desert. You must have read in the Old Testament how the people of Israel left Egypt, which symbolizes the sphere of evil, and Pharaoh, who symbolizes the devil; how the people of God fled from Egypt (evil) and Pharaoh (the tempter); how they crossed the Red Sea, arrived at Sinai, and lingered there for forty years, hopelessly lost. They simply wanted to go from Egypt to Palestine, a trip that shouldn't take much longer than two weeks.

Their desert sojourn has, in fact, a splendid spiritual meaning. Israel crossed the Red Sea, then immediately entered the desert: so did our Lord enter the desert immediately following His Baptism in the Jordan waters. You will recall St. Paul's words that God's people of old were *baptized* into Moses *in the Red Sea*: thus crossing the Red Sea is an Old Testament symbol of baptism. The people entered the Red Sea and emerged victorious against Pharaoh—who drowned in the sea, as Satan drowns in baptism. The Israelites' deliverance from Pharaoh is a symbol of the Church's deliverance from Satan. This is what Christ accomplished in the Jordan. He descended, with all of humanity in His heart and His side—just as in the vision of the girl we know, who dreamed of Christ taking a congregation into His side and bringing them out cleansed and purified. Indeed, all of humanity, and specifically you and I and every person now listening, "entered" into Christ when He was baptized in the Jordan. The entire Church was baptized in the Jordan and gained the victory over Satan.

"Then Jesus, being filled with the Holy Spirit, returned from the Jordan and was led by the Spirit into the wilderness"[1]—the Spirit of victory. Doesn't it amaze you that, after the victory of His Baptism, He enters the wilderness? Ah, but this reminds us of the Israelites' entrance into the wilderness, which became for them a trial. The Israelites were put to the test in the desert for forty years, just as the Lord was tested in the desert; however, only forty days were needed for Him—Christ's forty days typify the Israelites' forty years. And you

---

1   Luke 4:1

will be astounded to discover that the temptations were the same in both cases.

THE FIRST TEMPTATION

The first temptation the people of Israel encountered was that of hunger and the stomach; round stones shaped like loaves were strewn everywhere. They scolded Moses and said, "Did you bring us to the desert to die? We hunger!" Temptation will always assault human nature at the time of fasting, and of worship, and of resistance to the desires of the flesh. The lust for food asserts itself against the stomach, the "Lord of Cravings," as it's known to monks. The first of all temptations meets us through the stomach. So the devil came to Christ and said, "Look, why don't You make one of these stones become bread?" The Israelites likewise went to Moses and said, "Will you kill us in the desert? We want to eat!" Then manna fell from heaven. But Christ is the true manna. And He is the bread from heaven—will *He* turn stones to bread?

Satan said, "If You are the Son of God, turn these stones into bread."

And now, after what I've explained, look how fine and wonderful is our Lord's response. He said, "Man shall not live by bread alone, but by every *word* that proceeds from the mouth of God." He is indicating Himself—the *Word*—He is the source of life, and the true bread from heaven, for which we have been praying liturgies for 1900 years and counting. This bread has sufficed all of humanity—every color, race, people, and nation under heaven—without being used up. And it will never, ever be depleted! He said "not by bread," which is made from wheat, which is pulled up from the ground among stones. Ground that is full of stones can actually be plowed, seeded, and watered, and it will produce wheat. Is it really that difficult to change stones to bread? Give me six months, with seeds, rocks, and water, and I'll produce some wheat for you. Christ says that life is not based on this type of bread or wheat, but on God's Word. And I imagine that he was pointing to Himself while saying, "every *word* that proceeds from the mouth of God."

So in truth, Christ Himself, on behalf of the entire Church, faced the trial which afflicted Israel in the desert and gained the victory over the stomach. Ah, how wonderful, how glorious! We thank You, our Lord Jesus Christ, for You have opened the doors of fasting to every person; and from You, Lord, we receive the strength to defeat the lust of food and the stomach! O You who fasted forty days and forty nights, for whom did You fast and for whom did You gain the victory, but for us, in order to grant us good things? Grant good things to all Your people in Your Church, that they might realize the power in fasting, that each person might fast and depend on Your strength. O Lord, we thank You, for the Church has bequeathed to us this strength in the mystery of the Great Fast.

This was the first temptation, which our Lord defeated on a collective and individual level, to give the Church a season of fasting replete with victory. But there are many who begin the fast tired and scared. Certain souls become overwhelmed, saying, "O Lord, will I be able to fast? I'm sick and fatigued. I work all day with my mind and standing on my two legs." Oh, do not fear! The Lord fasted; and when He fasted, He overcame; and when He overcame, He infused victory into fasting. Let us thank the Lord for giving us the ability to fast. And how beautiful is fasting with the reading of the Word! Now you can see the link between the two; what do we receive? Fullness! We are filled and watered on the spiritual level. As the book Wisdom of Sirach says, "He who eats me also hungers for me, and he who drinks me also thirsts for me." This, my beloved, was our Lord's experience during the forty days, which the Church assimilated for herself.

What do you think would have happened if the people of Israel hadn't complained in the desert? They would have lived the entire forty years praising God and blessing the Most High. They stumbled, however; but God has overcome the stumbling block. As St. Paul says, "Your fathers tested me in the desert forty years."[2] And sadly, their corpses fell—six hundred thousand souls—because of lack of faith, because of complaining, because of disobedience to God's word! They buried the corpses in the sand and moved on; and finally, Moses saw the land afar off, but neither did he enter. Only Caleb and Joshua made it, out of six hundred thousand people. Why all these dead? As St. Paul says, it was because of their faithlessness.

Again, why did the Lord fast forty days and forty nights? We know that He was baptized, and His baptism granted the Church power and renewal, a new creation, and the work of the Holy Spirit. The Cross lifted from humanity its sin, cleansed it, and purified it; and the Resurrection raised us from spiritual death to eternal life. So our Lord's fasting redeemed us from the first fault committed by humanity during its training in the desert—that is, complaining, hunger, and testing God. The Lord overcame the "Lord of Cravings," which has caused many to stumble and has distanced them from holiness, the Church, and God.

"Man shall not live by bread alone but by every word of God"— these words should ring not only in your ears but in your hearts also. Never forget them; engrave them on your hearts. Of course, Satan thought Christ would be easy to defeat and did not understand that He was the very Word and source of life, the bread come down from heaven. This is the mystical bread of which all humanity partakes, yet is never filled, and always returns for more, as Jesus the son of Sirach says, "He who eats me returns to me hungry again." For 1900 years the Church has been eating this heavenly bread: is she "full"? Every Sunday, Wednesday, Friday, along with the rest of the week, she eats of

---

2   Heb 3:9

this bread, then returns the following week and finds it again present on the altar. And every person who eats this bread hungers more for it.

THE SECOND TEMPTATION

We can now speak about the second temptation. Satan took Him atop the wings of the temple, which overhung and overlooked the Kidron Valley, and below that was a vast area of land, full of people and towns. Satan told Him, "Show to everyone that You will jump in greatness from the wings of the temple; and when You descend among the people, they will applaud You. And this is actually not a 'temptation' at all; for it's written in the Psalms that the angels will take care of You in Your descent, and not a stone will injure Your foot. Isn't this psalm written specifically for You? 'For He shall give His angels charge over you, to keep you in all your ways. In their hands they shall bear you up, lest you dash your foot against a stone' (Ps 91:11, 12)." Marvel at the devil's devious skill in selecting verses! Yes, most frightful is the devil's skill in using Bible verses!

But in Deuteronomy we also have this: "You shall not tempt the Lord your God" (Deut 6:16). What, O Lord, does it mean not to tempt the Lord your God? If we go back to the case of the Israelites in the desert, it will shed some light on the meaning. Moses went up on the mountain to fast and speak with God; and the people suspected Moses during those forty days. They said, "What, is there something wrong with this God? Maybe He delays too long and is not true to His word. Maybe this God is just not for us."

Notice the same words might arise from you—"God makes a lot of promises but doesn't come through. He's too patient and takes too long in everything. I don't know if He can save or deliver me. Maybe He's just not for me."

So the people said, "Let's make another god. A pleasant god—one we can see, shining and dazzling, to make us happy. Who has nice earrings and bracelets?" They gathered all the gold—and *who* made for them the calf? Would you believe it? They said to *Aaron*, "Make us a calf to worship—a dazzling, beautiful calf, before which we can feast and rejoice."

Oh, for this tempting of God! This second temptation is directly offensive to God Himself. Why? Because, if a person flies down from the wings of the temple with his arms extended, effecting a stunning sight—whose glory is he stealing? God's glory, without question. The second temptation which meets a man is that of tempting God by usurping His honor. The first temptation is quite natural, in that it targets the stomach; it is the easy temptation, by which Satan throws in his fishing line and pulls out a thousand souls at once. The second temptation is a harder sell; it involves the person who has managed to fulfill his hungers and physical needs and so begins going to church and living religiously. Once he's in church, he sees the congregation around him and says to himself, "I should be more recognized here. I'm a man of position." Then they elevate him because of his murmuring and pestering; and thence he continues to demand higher and higher promotions.

The bitter second temptation—the temptation of the golden calf—is the temptation to come down from the wings of the temple to earn the applause of people! We desire to mingle with people as individuals of distinction; but, my Lord, it is not our own honor—it is stolen from God! "So-and-so is a public official." "So-and-so is a great hermit." "So-and-so possesses a revered name." Oh, woe is me if I steal God's honor! Woe is me if I climb the temple to steal His glory!

The priesthood itself—with its large hats and shining robes, and its hands and feet constantly kissed by the laity—is severely tried by this temptation.

"Why, O father priest, are you upset?"

"They insulted my dignity and honor. I'm a priest of God! How could they do this to me? I must look after God's honor which is *in me.*"

I fear, oh I fear this second temptation, which maims and gathers up its victims, great and small. Even the woman who is given a service in the church becomes puffed up. "This is the priest's wife." "This is a group leader." "This is the one in charge over all Sunday school." "This woman is a talented preacher." "What a woman for saving souls!" And she begins walking about as if she were a god. Then she begins falling into sins which were not previously a problem. Why? Because she stole God's honor. Anger, jealousy, spite, judging, and all sorts of evils enter, because God has withdrawn Himself. Oh, what a bitter temptation!

If you paid attention to what is written in the Catholic Epistle for today, you'd be amazed and know that the one who arranged these readings was truly filled with the Holy Spirit. It says, "My brethren, do not hold the faith of our Lord Jesus Christ, the Lord of glory, with partiality. For if there should come into your assembly a man with gold rings, in fine apparel, and there should also come in a poor man in filthy clothes, and you pay attention to the one wearing the fine clothes and say to him, 'You sit here in a good place,' and say to the poor man, 'You stand there,' or, 'Sit here at my footstool'" (James 2:1–3).

It's like saying, "Excuse me, sir, what brought you to this church here today?"

"Isn't today Sunday?"

"I know today is Sunday, so what? I mean what brings you here among these people?"

"Don't they pray on Sunday?"

"Yes, and so what?"

"What, did I do something wrong? I have come to pray and take Communion."

"Yes, but . . . you're not dressed properly."

"Oh, but I'm a poor man; I don't have anything except this simple tunic."

These are the words of St. James. We all want to be great, important people; but then we reject the poor man dressed in simple clothing.

I fear that I am like this . . . O Lord, have mercy on me! O God, I fear that I am of this type! I told you before that by the first temptation, Satan throws in his fishing net and pulls up a thousand. Here he throws in the net, waits two, three, maybe ten days, then pulls up one fish—but a nice, big, fattened fish. My beloved, everyone who is given the service of the Word, or a position in the church, or a talent for hymns, is faced with this temptation. Anyone who stands at the pulpit, or speaks in a classroom, or takes up any large or small role in church, is tried by the temptation of the temple wings. O Jesus, You who in the verse in Deuteronomy opened the pages of Your heart, grant us never to tempt You. O Lord, give us a conscience that accepts the "lowest place,"[3] a conscience that considers the speaker less than the listeners, the hymn chanter less than the hearers, and the educated less than the unlearned!

THE THIRD TEMPTATION

The third temptation remains. The devil took Him by the mind's eye—a vision which spiritually is called the "logical" or "reasonable" vision—the ability of a person to see into the true essence of things. It's a vision which only some people have; but it's a sign neither of salvation nor godliness nor election. There are some people who have been given the ability by God to see the unseen—by the mind or heart.

Satan took Him by this spiritual vision up onto a high mountain, but it wasn't a physical mountain; it was a "spiritual" or "mental" mountain. He showed Him all the kingdoms of the world and their

---

3   Luke 14:10

authorities, and said, "I will give you all this, because it's mine." He pulled from his pocket—if you will imagine with me—a certificate saying that he is the Prince of This World, even with God's name stamped on it. He said, "If you doubt my words, here is proof from God that I am officially prince of this world. I own everything in it. And if You bow to me, I will give it to You. You can have it all without enduring the Cross or any other affliction. Don't you want to own the world with God as Your Father? It's very simply done—just worship me and all is Yours."

We return to the people of Israel and see an exact parallel. After the water flowed from the rock and manna fell from heaven, and life was fairly good, they said, "We've become strong; come, sharpen your swords! On we go to conquer! Once we reach Palestine, we will destroy every man and beast and possess the land!"

"We will *possess* . . ." Ah, he who falls into the first and second very easily falls into this third temptation. The Israelites became a violent and blood-seeking people; and after they had cut down so many nations, they killed the Messiah Himself.

David even, the best of them, the great prophet whose heart was like the heart of God, asked to build God's temple; but He said, "No, do not let your hands touch it, because they are covered in blood."[4] Such was this people, violent and bloody, due to their lust for domination. How terrible is the lust for domination by which Satan overcame them in olden times! And this desire continues to wreak havoc in the world until now.

We thank You, O Lord Jesus Christ, for You refused this temptation, and instead accepted the Cross as victory instead of defeat! Christ was lifted up on the Cross as a victor; to be slaughtered on the Cross was more preferable to Him than to rule over the world. Christ—the possession and glory of the Church! He is also the possession (that

---

4   1 Chr 22:8

transcends every thought) of every soul. Go now to any lover of Christ and ask him, "What possessions do you own at home?"

He will say, "I have the Lord."

"And what do you have in the bank?"

"I have the Lord." Even if he be renowned, he will desire no other possession but this.

I once asked a godly man, "I heard that you have lots of money; do you own this large villa you're living in?"

He said, "No."

"What? This villa isn't yours?"

"No."

"I'm dumbfounded. Why didn't you buy it with all your money?"

He said, "I made a promise to myself that I would not own a foot of earth. I desire to be unbound. And before I die, I will not own a single pound in the bank."

"Why, my friend?" I asked.

He said, "Because I used to desire all such things; but the day I possessed the Lord in my heart, all desire to own anything else vanished."

Blessed be the Lord Jesus Christ, who defeated Satan in this third ordeal on the high mountain! The mountain of possession and dominion, the mountain of the mind from which many of the world's great men have fallen and died! We do not own things, but things own us and exploit us! Everyone who owns a thousand pounds is not the ruler, but the slave, of a thousand pounds; and the one who owns ten thousand is the slave of ten thousand. My Lord, is it better to be the slave of one thousand or of ten thousand? The answer is clear: It's easier to be the servant of a thousand than of ten thousand. We thank You, our Lord Jesus Christ, for you have made us slaves to nobody. You freed us, and defeated for us the lust of the stomach, and the lust for honor, and have given us the freedom as sons!

Oh, how great is this trial which Christ entered into with Satan and conquered for us! The Church should never desire rule or ownership on earth. Woe to the church that possesses much! Woe to the church that has numerous investments stored away in the national and central banks, only to be eaten away by the moth! Woe to the church whose assets are large while her poor are hungry! Woe to the church which owns many acres and buildings but has no poor eating at her table! But blessed is the church which is satisfied with Christ the Word, and gives daily from her riches, that the people might claim ownership with her in heaven—possessions which cannot be buried, pass away, or perish. They are preserved for the last day. Blessed be the Lord Jesus Christ, who gained for us this third victory, and granted us to be poor on the outside; but we are rich with possessions greater than all the stuff of this world.

O You, our Lord Jesus Christ, who lived poor but are the King of kings! O You who defeated Satan in the battle of the Kingdom and the battle for worldly glory, and granted us the elect poverty, that we might live in Your wealth forever, an unshakable wealth! Grant us, O Son of God, to overcome in this third trial, to live and die for You. We are sons of the Kingdom, sons of light, and will walk under Your rule. Bless us, O Lord, as a Church and as individuals. O You who conquered for us, make us into a strong and glorious Church without blemish! And let each of us rejoice in You as overcomers in this third trial, and leave here knowing that we have a victorious nature in You, O Son of God. Bless us, and may Your name be glorified in Your Church both now and forever. Amen.

On the Canaanite Woman

A s you know, brethren, we are in the season of Holy Great Lent, in which Christ accomplished for us a great and astounding victory over the enemy. We must be very attentive, brethren, to the Scripture readings so we may be able to understand why this part of the Gospel was chosen for this day.

> *Then Jesus went out from there and departed to the region of Tyre and Sidon. And behold, a woman of Canaan came from that region and cried out to Him, saying, "Have mercy on me, O Lord, Son of David! My daughter is severely demon-possessed." But He answered her not a word. And His disciples came and urged Him, saying, "Send her away, for she cries out after us." But He answered and said, "I was not sent except to the lost sheep of the house of Israel." Then she came and worshiped Him, saying, "Lord, help me!" But He answered and said, "It is not good to take the children's bread and throw it to the little dogs." And she said, "Yes, Lord, yet even the*

*little dogs eat the crumbs which fall from their masters' table." Then
Jesus answered and said to her, "O woman, great is your faith! Let it
be to you as you desire." And her daughter was healed from that very
hour. (Matt 15:21–28, NKJV)*

St. Matthew summarizes the story very briefly in his Gospel, but
St. Mark makes things clearer with a few details: "And He entered a
house and wanted no one to know *it*, but He could not be hidden."[1] So
He went into this far country apparently in desire of a quiet retreat.
And He most probably told the disciples, "Please do not indicate My
whereabouts to anyone who comes looking for Me. I am in need of
rest." In other words, it was His clear intent to be in concealment for a
time. So He entered a house and locked Himself in.

But then "a woman whose young daughter had an unclean spirit
heard about Him, and she came and fell at His feet."[2] Strange thing!
Tyre and Sidon were, of course, geographically detached from
Jerusalem and paid no allegiance to that city. They were Canaanites,
the descendants of the Philistines, who had never felt any inclination
toward Israel, and from the time Israel first entered Palestine until
the end of Solomon's reign had never bowed to Israel's rule. So there
existed a natural division between Tyre and Sidon, and Israel. How
strange it is, then, that Christ would travel all the way to Tyre and
Sidon and choose a house there to enter and rest!

Then a woman finds him whom the Gospel specifically marks out
as a Canaanitess—not one of God's people—a Gentile. I want to
resolve here a big problem which confronts every reader and preacher
of this passage—that she came to Christ requesting Him to heal her
daughter, and He told her that He could not take the children's bread
and throw it to the little dogs. Every person who reads this stumbles!

---

1   Mark 7:24
2   Mark 7:25

"Christ never said anything like this!" they say, "and it isn't equal to Him." Wonder! O Lord, what is the meaning of this? Before I begin to explain the entire passage, this verse must be vindicated, or we will be prevented from understanding the whole. If we understand this verse and restore it to its rightful place, we will rejoice greatly, be greatly comforted, and also be greatly strengthened.

We must begin to understand why the Holy Spirit through St. Matthew mentions Tyre and Sidon and the Canaanite woman together. Tyre and Sidon were (as we said) old Canaanite cities before Israel entered the land, and they remained afterward religiously independent and worshiped foreign gods. They especially worshiped a god named Baal. He was the chief god of the Canaanites, as well as of the Canaanite woman. Tyre, where this woman lived, was the center of Baal worship. You will remember that the house of Jezebel, wife of King Ahab who brought darkness on Israel, was made into a center for Baal worship. You will also remember the dramatic exchange between Jezebel and Elijah. Baal's priests were four hundred in number; and Elijah, the servant of Jehovah, stood before them and said, "We will offer a sacrifice and see whom God answers." Of course He heard Elijah, and a great fire from heaven descended and consumed the sacrifice as well as the four hundred priests of Baal.

I say all this for an important reason. Baal, which means "lord," was worshiped upon the high places;[3] and the "high place" was called *zebul* in the Assyrian or Canaanite language. So their god was called "lord of the high places," or *Baalzebul*—so you've just learned another name for Satan. Satan used to enter their idols and perform tricks to cause the people to stray. Since the Jews loved to ridicule the pagan idols, they found a word in their own language, *zebub*, which meant "flies"— very near our *zubab* in Arabic—and in mockery of the Canaanites, the Israelites called that idol *Baalzebub*, "lord of the flies." In any Jewish

---

3   1 Kin 12:31

manuscript you will find the word *Baalzebub* and never *Baalzebul*, while in every Canaanite or Syro-Phoenician manuscript you will find written *Baalzebul*. Remember that when they wanted to insult Christ for casting out demons, they told Him, "You cast out demons by Baalzebub, the ruler of the demons."[4]

Now, this woman was a Canaanite who worshipped Baalzebul. So what did Baalzebul's worship look like? It was a base and depraved worship, one which distorted human nature through its obscenities. I cannot say more than that it was an unclean religion. Human bodies were subjected to the filthiest abuses in honor of this god. They even slaughtered children in offering to Baal, which is mentioned in the Old Testament.[5]

We have neared our answer. Christ did not go easy at all on the Canaanite woman's religion. The basis of the Jewish sacrificial system was the lamb, a simple, pure animal—an expression of a pure sacrifice. The Jews used to signify the unclean worship of paganism, even unto today, by the image of the dog, which is the animal symbol of uncleanness. This was true to the extent that if a dog's tail touched a clean Jew, he would be rendered unclean and go immediately to bathe.

Now He told her, "Woman, it is not good to take the children's bread and throw it to the dogs." Here He exposes the vile depths of her worship; He uncovers the sordid depths of her life. She was not just offering lip-service worship to Baalzebul but participating to the fullest degree. I don't think there was any accusation here, and the Canaanite woman did not feel that Christ was scolding her. But we'll see how she accepted Christ's words to herself; and they apply not just to her, believe me, but also to you and me, and even to David the Prophet.[6] Every person who knows himself to be unclean will stand

---

4   Luke 11:14
5   Jer 32:35
6   1 Sam 24:14

before God and say, "I am like a dog." So when the Lord referred to the woman with this title, he was not scolding, and neither did she feel it so; but it was the simple truth.

I have now begun to feel relief at putting to rest this verse which has so troubled its readers—that Christ, in his kindness, delicacy, and immeasurable compassion, would say to one supplicating Him in tears for her daughter a verse that seems at first glance inappropriate to Him. I have insisted in refuting the errors that have accumulated about this verse and in restoring to Christ His rightful place.

When the Canaanite woman went to request that Christ heal her daughter, what exactly would be this "healing"? A mere passing word? You forget that when the woman with a flow of blood[7] approached Christ and touched Him, and hid herself, He said, "Power has gone out from Me."[8] Ah, thank God, I am arriving at something here.

So what did the Canaanitess request of Christ? *Power.* Could it be just a trifling word that would heal her daughter? No—His word draws out *power.* She is simply incapable of forming a right estimate of her request; she doesn't realize what she's asking for! She says, "Heal my daughter," and imagines that the healing is an easy thing. She thought it might be as easy as making a cake for Baal—as we read in the Old Testament that they served Asthoreth[9]—according to her pagan worship.

Christ wanted to show her that this healing would be founded upon the death of the Cross; upon sacrifice and redemption; upon a holy Body offered up to the Father; upon a living sacrifice for sinners. "Do you know that you are requesting none other than My Cross? And you are requesting the Body that will be fixed to it. It is not by a fleeting word that I heal your daughter, but by My death. It is by the

---

7   Matt 9, Mark 5, Luke 8
8   Luke 8:46
9   Judg 10:6

Bread of Life that comes down from heaven—the children's Bread." You understand of course that I am speaking in symbols. "You are requesting the Bread of heaven, which all who eat of it are healed. Can I offer you My Body, when you just the other day made a cake for Baal and offered it with filthy rites?" Now you see the meaning—"Can I take the children's bread and offer it to dogs?" I have now exhausted the verse, so we may begin to learn the whole passage.

So, what is our portion in this Gospel passage? It's very, very great indeed! I tell you, not one person will leave the church today, not even the smallest and weakest soul, without carrying with him a large and robust store of faith—thanks to this amazing Canaanite woman. I'd like to return to our beloved St. Mark:

> He arose and went to the region of Tyre and Sidon. And He entered
> a house and wanted no one to know it, but He could not be hidden.
> For a woman whose young daughter had an unclean spirit heard
> about Him, and she came and fell at His feet.[10]

Pay attention, because the path that Christ will walk now with the Canaanite woman is extremely important, for it's the same path He walks with us. Pay very close attention. He is doing things that outwardly we wouldn't have expected. It seems at first that He is in an isolated retreat and desires nobody to approach Him. She had been asking for days and weeks about the Messiah of the Jews: "Has He come to these parts yet?"

"No, ma'am."

"He didn't come last week?"

"No."

"But I heard that He was on the road to Tyre and Sidon, and I'm waiting for Him." She probably even went to Israel in search of Him.

---

10   Mark 7:24, 25

But she was a Gentile, a servant of Baalzebul, a worshipper of idols, unclean, and according to the Jews a "dog." But oh, what good this "dog" will do for us today!

She had learned that He was residing in the house in secret; so she stood without and was crying, "Have mercy on me, O Lord, Son of David!"

You can imagine Christ's response to the disciples: "What, did any of you tell her that I am here?"

They said, "Not at all!" She was a relentless woman—she would keep requesting till she received!

I imagine that Peter first went out to her. "What do you want, ma'am?"

"I want to see the Son of David."

He said, "The Son of David doesn't meet with anyone. Go now from here."

She said, "I'm not leaving. I want to see the Lord, the Son of David."

He said, "It is impossible that He see anyone now."

She answered, "I tell you I will see Him!" At this point she began to cry out, "O Lord, Son of David, have mercy on me!"

Peter repeated, "Listen to me: He will not see you, He will not hear you, ever!"

Then John went out, with his calm and polite manner, and told her, "Ma'am, please listen to Peter; he's our elder brother, and his word is set and immovable. He will not meet with you."

She responded, "Young man, put yourself at rest. I will see Him!" You see that it wasn't for nothing that she would be finally commended for her great faith.

Then Christ came out and stood before her without uttering a word. All this time she had been crying out, "Lord, Son of David, my daughter is severely demon-possessed. Have mercy on me!"

He was silent while she cried and wailed, as the disciples stood looking on. He said to them, "I was not sent except to the lost sheep of Israel."

So the disciples agreed and repeated to the woman, "Woman, you hear what He says."

She said, "Put yourselves at rest," and began to prostrate herself while wailing even louder.

Of course, she had made such a scene by now that a crowd was gathering around them. The disciples said to Him, "Send her away, for she cries out after us. Just give her a word so that she leaves!" Behold the state of these disciples, whom He would one day send out to evangelize the world!

She threw herself at His feet and said, "Lord, help me!" He made as if He hadn't heard. She persisted with repeated bows and supplications. What would you expect from the poor mother? Her daughter was demon-possessed and wearied her every day at home; she couldn't bear her life any longer.

She was extremely weary and downcast—just like you all, my mothers and my sisters. How often older siblings or parents come to me with tears in their eyes and exclaim, "Father, I am so tired. My daughter is going down the wrong way." Or, "Father, my son, whom I brought up, is going astray." They come to me, but what can I do for them? Did the Canaanite woman go to Peter or John? Did the disciples form a prayer meeting for her? No, she went to Christ and said, "Lord, help me!"

The first stage of Christ's actions was to make as if He would meet with noone; the second stage was to go out and say in her hearing, "I was not called except to the lost sheep of Israel," meaning that her request was out of place and that He could not help her.

Then she began to bow to Him frantically—a direct act of worship—and say, "Lord, help me. Help me!"

The third stage, which was the great trial, was when He said, "It is not good to take the children's bread and throw it to the little dogs."

We've already agreed that this remark had no harshness in it but that she understood His meaning. And what did this remarkable woman say? "Yes, it's true." She did not pity herself or grow angry. "It's true, I do not deserve to eat the children's bread, and I would never dare to sit at their table. But it is not a full loaf that I request, but only the crumbs."

Christ had desired this from her from the first. Why did He delay so long inside? Why did He make the point about coming only for the lost sheep of Israel? And why did He refuse to give the children's bread to the little dogs? He did so in order to burst open the well of faith in her, that we might drink of it all our lives!

She didn't say, "Yes Lord, *but* the little dogs eat the crumbs . . ." There is no "but" in the original Greek. She said, "Yes Lord, *and* the little dogs eat . . ." She is saying, "All that You say is true; but Your words still give me hope, because the dogs can eat from the falling crumbs. I might not be worthy to eat directly from Your hand, or the children's hands; but the dogs can still eat the crumbs."

Then Christ spoke to her those great words, which were not said to any other person all the prior years He dwelt on earth: "O woman, great is your faith! Let it be to you as you desire." He says, "All that you have desired is now yours." The devil can never endure a faith of this magnitude.

I want to recapitulate to refocus on the Canaanite woman's actions so that we may begin to draw lessons from the story. Was it possible for her to expend any more effort in endeavoring to meet Christ and present to Him her plea? No—she did all. She was a Canaanitess; and as we said, the Canaanites were enemies to the Jews, because the Jews took their land, Palestine, resulting in a bitter enmity between the two. Canaan was the son of Ham. Ham had done a vile thing against

his father, Noah[11]—which also involved impurity and uncleanliness—
and thus Noah placed a curse upon his choicest son, Canaan.[12]

The Canaanite woman was aware of her background, and as it
was written in the Torah, she was an accursed daughter. She had no
right to any blessing. But did this stop her? Never. Not one bit! She
didn't care about her deprivation of the Jewish blessing. And did she
care, or did shame stop her, because she was a worshipper of a pagan
god, Baalzebul? No—but she approached Him and said, "O Son of
David!" Or did she heed when they told her, "He's in seclusion now"?
Not at all. Or was she stopped by Christ's words when He said, "I'm
not for you. I came only for the lost sheep of Israel"? No—rather she
pushed all the more. Was she dissuaded when Christ told her she was
of a rejected people? Did she regard any of these things? Never. Oh,
amazing thing! Amazing, I say, is this woman's faith!

What was it then, my brethren, that supported this woman? What
did she have to depend on? Did she have a promise or covenant to lean
on? Did she have a written Scripture or Law to trust in? Did she rest
upon any personal right she had? She knew herself—as every sinner
knows himself—to be without any right to approach God; and yet she
approached! Did she have hope in any good she had done? Did she
have an intercessor to plead on her behalf? Did she have a priest to
offer a sacrifice for her? Nothing at all.

Then what was it that strengthened her? She looked unto Christ—
and Christ alone. She focused all her faith, her mind, and her heart on
Him. She trusted, not because she had anything to commend her, but
because *He* had all things. She depended not upon her own strength
but upon His. She did not lean upon any promise she had, but upon
the promise found in Him. When she said, "Son of David," she meant
to remind Him of the promises that foretold Him as Messiah.

---

11   Gen 9:21–23
12   Gen 9:24

Remember, beloved, when a faith leans not upon self but upon Christ, and is not supported by any personal credentials or rights but by those of Christ, and is not backed by any good works done by self or by ancestors—yet if such a faith is still strong, isn't it equal to the truth in Christ? For if I depend on myself even a little, then I must decrease Christ's portion in the work. Why? Because I can say, "I have done this for You." Then I will proceed to say, "I'm not like the rest of sinners; I fast twice a week and give tithes of all my money"—you remember the story.[13] Why, that person[14] removed God completely from his good works!

But this woman said, "I am truly a little dog, and I have no right to You. But You are rich. You have all, and give all, and are all. I am coming to *You*, not to *me*." She raised her faith to the level of Christ. Isn't this a clear glorification of Christ?

He told her, "Great is your faith!" What is "great" faith, my beloved, but the faith that equals the stature of Christ? Maybe the lesson here is hard; but I think that anyone who pays due attention will grasp it. "Little" faith is that which isn't equal to Christ; and we'll see an example presently. But the mystery of great faith is that which is lifted to the level of Christ Himself—which is given to us on this blessed day through this Gospel. Thus was the faith of this Canaanite woman, who trusted in nothing in herself or in all of humanity. Her faith was lifted so high, to Christ's own level, that He could see Himself in it!

No one on earth had ever before heard the words spoken to him, "Great is your faith." We've only heard those other words, "O you of little faith; why did you doubt?"[15] And wasn't this said to Peter, the strong, preeminent leader of the disciples, whom Christ charged to strengthen the brethren and feed His sheep?[16] Our Gospel reading

---

13   Luke 18:9–14
14   The Pharisee
15   Matt 14:31
16   John 21:17

for today comes from Matthew 15, but the incident with Peter is found right before in Matthew 14, where he says to Christ, "If You are the Lord, command me to come to You on the water," and Christ answers, "Come."

He walked a little and found winds blowing—not the forsakenness of Tyre and Sidon and of being a Gentile, but just a strong wind—and he feared, and sank, and said, "Lord, help me!"

Christ told him, "O you of little faith."

If we had a Canaanite woman in the Church today, we would see like great faith, instead of the doubt that plagues the Church in every place and every heart; and she would lift from the Church the burden of impurity which is filling our streets. Why are you despondent, my mother and my sister, coming with tears in your eyes? "My daughter, my daughter! Satan has deceived her and she is going down the wrong path."

"My sister, have you heard about the Canaanite woman?"

"Who is that?"

Go, read the Gospel, and you will see one who had nothing to hope in but went directly to Christ. Satan could not prevent her, for she said, "I seek the Messiah." The disciples themselves tried to block her way because she wasn't of their people. "I tried Ashtoreth," she said, "but that availed nothing; and now I seek Him whom they call the Son of David. I know for certain that He will grant healing." My sister, have you seen this Canaanitess, who had nothing and nobody to hope in? Nothing at all can prevent you from going to Christ in power! Know that nobody can hinder you, not even an angel, just as Paul says that no angel can separate us from the Gospel.[17]

Though the time fails me, I would also like to relate this story to the temptation on the Mount. Satan tried to defeat Christ, but Satan himself was defeated by this woman! How wonderful, O Lord, how

---

17 Rom 8:35

wonderful! You descended from the mountain after the forty days and gave all humanity power to defeat Satan. O Canaanite woman, where did you get your power? Ah, Christ gave it to all humans; and so the Canaanitess was able to defeat Satan, my beloved, and break him!

O Lord, You are glorious! The forty days You spent in the wilderness were not in vain; but You overcame for the sake of the Canaanite woman, and for every slave and freeman. To every nation on earth You have given this victory over Satan! We, with the Canaanitess's tongue, preach to all the earth that it is within everyone's power to defeat the enemy—by faith. By the faith that rests on nothing but Christ's righteousness and authority.

She was not worthy of the crumbs that fall from the children's table, but she left not only with the children's bread, but with something even greater. Peter, who was a choice "son," was told in the previous chapter, "O you of little faith." He made himself a big shot. Why, if the other eleven were in the boat, did he have to walk on the water? He felt he had something more than the other disciples; and for this he sank.

If we feel we have something that raises us above our brother, we will receive nothing. We have before us this great example, Peter, who is not a small biblical figure, but even raised the dead.[18] He trusted in himself, he sank, and he heard the bitter rebuke, "O you of little faith, why did you doubt?" Beloved, I beseech you to pay attention to the Gospel of this day, and that you remember what I have said, that whenever you stand to pray and think yourself better than any person around, you will receive nothing. Or at most you may hear, "O you of little faith."

"Let it be to you as you desire." A great gift—and He gave her many other things besides. Do not suppose that she remained a Canaanitess. She went rather to fetch her daughter, and they both became followers of Christ. No one who tastes Christ can ever leave Him again! "He

18 Acts 9:36–43

who eats of Me returns hungering again," as is written in the Wisdom of Jesus Son of Sirach; and "He who drinks Me returns thirsting again." Ah, the Canaanite woman could never again live without Him; and she remains forever inspiring the faith of the Church. Did we not even today receive spiritual blessings on her account? We partook of the children's bread although unworthy.

Oh, for Your glory, Lord Jesus Christ! Our righteous God, this blessed people which has come out into the desert to eat the children's bread, grant them to be filled! Grant them a faith that will satisfy all their desire in You! Give to every woman anguishing on account of her daughter, and to every father anguishing on account of a son or brother, the Canaanite woman's faith. Bless us; for Yours is the glory, power, and honor in Your Church, both now and forever. Amen.

On the Epistle to the Romans

1973

A spiritual epistle: let us meditate together, and we will soon see how it should be read. I will proceed word by word, as does a person who opens the Bible looking for comfort. You have all grown accustomed to reading a chapter in an hour, or maybe a half-hour; but you will now see us taking a lengthy period to cover three or four verses—for this is true reading. The other method of reading, which takes only a short time, is a mere reading for mental knowledge or rational criticism. But our reading ought to be *foundational*—that is, we are founding our minds on Christ's words uttered by Paul.

"Paul, a bondservant of Jesus Christ, called to be an apostle" (Rom 1:1). The Apostle Paul here describes himself as "bondservant." O Lord Jesus, I wish to be Your bondservant—what do You say? Did You not let the Apostle Paul write this epistle, my Lord, and have You not preserved it these long years, that it might reach me? I am confident, O Lord, that this epistle has reached me that I might take in, comprehend, and feel every word. Grant me therefore, O Lord, to receive exactly what we read.

Paul—ah, I wish to be like Paul!—You chose from the midst of the world, and he became an example to all Christians. At first he was very distant from You: a scoundrel, a haughty Pharisee, and a persecutor of the Church, besides other things. I am not much better than He was, so it is not a hard thing for me to be like Paul. I *wish* to be like Paul! At the very least, my Lord, I want to be like Paul in his understanding of You, and in his love for Your Gospel, and in his desire and toil for Your honor. See, Lord, Paul calls himself Your bondservant—and I also want to be Your bondservant. Would you permit me, Lord, to make a covenant with You now to be Your bondservant? I do not wish to be a servant of the world. O Lord, the world has enslaved many and put them in a daze, has distanced them from You and made their lives lost. But I wish to be Your bondservant, to live for You and die for You, as the Apostle Paul did.

So make this day a day of salvation for me, O Lord, and this hour an hour of salvation, that I might make a new covenant with You. I do not desire to be free, my Lord. Everything that is offered me in life, I resolve not to use by my own freedom. I have given myself many liberties for many long years; and when I gave myself such liberties, did I not stray far from You, Lord? I want to live as Your bondservant, and my desire is not to sense my personal freedom again. I will bind myself to be a servant who follows You: I will do nothing without Your counsel, and I will not begin any work unless I feel Your will and shepherding in it. Remember what he writes in his epistles: "I desired to go north to Macedonia, but the Spirit forbade me";[1] and, "I wanted to go down, but the Spirit forbade me"; and then he saw a vision, "Come over to Macedonia and help us;"[2] and, "When I was

---

1   Acts 16:6
2   Acts 16:9

going through Jerusalem, the Spirit told me to do such and such."[3] He was living by the Spirit of God, and the Spirit of God was working in him abundantly.

Paul was once a Pharisee and so considered himself the chief of sinners. And rightly so, for every Pharisee who held to the letter of the law produced a long list of sins: pride, self-admiration, and all else. But from the day the Apostle Paul enslaved himself to the Lord Jesus, he felt himself incapable of saying or doing anything without the Lord's permission and command; and he became a chosen vessel.

O Lord Jesus, I desire to be a chosen vessel. Is it too much for me? I am a foul person; but I know that the worse a person is, the more rightly does he become a chosen vessel. For when a bad vessel is put into Your hands, You make it new again. But if it is just half-good and half-bad, You simply repair the bad half. I am *all* bad. So I desire Your finger—that sharp, splendid, and beautiful finger—to touch upon every part of my body, mind, and nerves to make me a new vessel.

"Called to be an apostle." Ah! My Lord, You astonish me! A person who is far from You, a persecutor of the Church, corrupt in every sense of the word, and a good-for-nothing, is suddenly called to be an apostle? What benevolence is this, pray tell me, O my God! How rich is the call, that you would call and give and fill up so generously; and that such a vile person, a blood-shedder, should be called—and all at once to be an apostle? My goodness!

Look, I could never be like Paul. My days are unprofitable, not as those of Paul. All I can say is that if You call me in truth, and if You fill me with truth, and if You are surely willing to choose me for Yourself and make a covenant of my servitude to You—then, see Lord, the day You choose me to be Your messenger, I will not refuse, nor will I confer with flesh and blood.[4] I will become, O Lord, a herald for Your name

---

3   See Acts 21:14.
4   Gal 1:16

in every place and time; but all I want is for You to go with me just as You went with Paul.

Firstly, that You would let me feel that my life has truly changed in Your hands, and that the scales of sin and uncleanness would fall from my eyes as they fell from Paul's eyes. For what was it that blinded Paul? Sin. But when the divine light, the light of Jesus' face, encountered the sin in his eyes, it blinded him. He couldn't see. If his eyes had been wholesome, spiritual eyes, opened to the Gospel, he wouldn't have gone blind. But since his life was full of sin and haughtiness, his eyes were blinded in their clash with the light. They led him by the hand while his eyes were open, but he could see nothing.

He then was baptized by Ananias—that fine and meek apostle discreetly hidden in the Gospel. Once he laid hands on Paul, the scales fell from his eyes. Oh, my Lord, those hands have been laid on me many times, but the scales remain! And they will remain till the day of repentance, when they are shed by tears. My eyes are full of scales, O Son of God; and the day is needed when they shall be burst and reveal the springs of my eyes. The scales will fall, and sight will be restored to the eyes; and it is then that we will see You, O Son of God, in Your truth.

When I see Your meekness, never will I be haughty again. To this day, I still feel my pride and ego, and that I am something considerable among my brethren and those I serve—because I still do not see You clearly. But I am confident, O Son of God, that today my eyes will encounter Yours, and I will see humility in Your beautiful and luminous face. The scales will drop and the tears will fall.

From now on, never will I be seen again except with tears, or prostrate, or engaged in the service of the least. I will now choose the despised works—I, who used to seek the preeminence—I, who used to shun the weak and despised things—I, who would be enraged unless I had done the greatest works. I used to seek for myself the first place,[5] or at least the place next to the first. Once a gathering was assembled, my eyes would fall on the first place; and I would find a position which procured for me the most visibility. Ah, my Lord, the scales still remain! I promise You, Lord, that the day You send me the tears of true repentance, and I see Your face, never again will the world see me chasing after the first place or the greater work. And from under the throne, not on the throne, will I serve all the days of my life.

"Called to be an apostle." As you called Paul to be an apostle, I here place myself under Your will—send me. Send me, O Lord! All whom You choose, I am confident, You make capable of bearing the Word, and of bearing Your Person, to others. The desire of my heart, O Lord, when I read Your Gospel—as a novice servant—is that You use me for your Gospel, for the message of salvation, for the word of eternal life, and for the rich exposition of Your Word. I am still a beginner; all the doors before me are closed, and I do not know where to find the keys. Give unto me, O Lord, the keys to Your Gospel.

I promise You that in the day I feel Your Bible has opened up before me, I will not overrate my abilities, knowledge, or achievements, nor will I overvalue my position in the family as the firstborn and eldest, or my position in society as a professional, nor will I enlarge myself as a person well spoken of as having a grand future. God forbid! Rather, I wrap all things into a small bundle and place it at Your feet, saying, "Send me!" Henceforth, O Lord, I want to feel Your work in me and Your call to me. My heart is ready, O Lord; but it is in need of Your work. I set the Apostle Paul as an example before me day by day, for he said, "Imitate me, just as I also imitate Christ."[6]

Open my heart today, O Lord, that I might read and feel every single verse. For every verse holds a sign for me, and every word is sent to me by the Holy Spirit—to *me*, Lord, not just to the general public. I

---

5 See Luke 14:7–11.
6 1 Cor 1:11

read so that every word might be transformed into life for me. I do *not* read merely to become an expert in the Bible, or to stand and preach in church—God forbid! No, my Lord, this is not my task. My first duty is to live out Your Gospel, to live out these sweet verses, to rejoice in them, and to feel that You have truly selected me. And the mark of selection is Your hand that corrects, that strikes and heals, that presses and breaks, to make me new. After all this, then will I truly feel that You have chosen me and called me to be Your messenger.

"Separated to the gospel of God." There are many services, my beloved, which you might be called to; but there is none that equals the service of the Word. If, for example, you are called to serve the poor, halfway there you might feel the ego rising. A poor man or woman calls upon you for help, and you begin to feel yourself a bishop. You've become a big shot. And so it is with any other service.

But the service of the Word comforts and disciplines. As you read, you find the words striking back at you. You say, "My, this verse is against me; I must amend myself!" The service of the Word, or the study of the Gospel, for one's life, is a work which sustains itself. You read perhaps a certain passage which rebukes you, and you emerge after many days or months disciplined by the Word. Truly, to read a verse and say, "This verse is for me," is better than a thousand sermons.

This verse is placed here for me, O Lord, and I must amend myself. I cannot live while this verse is in the Bible! O Lord Jesus, please annul this verse and remove it from the Bible—would You allow me to cross it out? Of course He won't allow it. But my life is contrary to this verse, and I can't live while it remains! Either I change myself or the verse must go—then I must change myself. You must "run after" or pursue the verse, day by day and with tears, until you begin to change.

"Be transformed by the renewing of your minds."[7] Who or what can change the mind? The reading of the Word. "Separated to the

---

7   Rom 12:2

gospel of God." *The Gospel of God.* Ah, this is *Your* personal book. If I open this particular Bible, O Lord, and find written in it the owner's name, I say, "Oh, so-and-so gave me this Bible long ago; how dear is this Bible to me! So-and-so gave it to me on a great occasion, the day I started my church service." Or maybe, "The priest gave it to me on my wedding day. Ah, what precious memories! I could never forget the original giver."

Imagine every time you open your Bible to read, and kiss it as God's Bible, it is as a gift Christ sent down from heaven. The rock they brought from the moon is sold for a quarter or half a million pounds per kilogram. A large sum for a rock! The rocks we have here are better, but the moon rocks are sold at an exorbitant price per gram. Why? Because it's from the moon. This Bible is a rock that has fallen from heaven—from God's bosom, from God's Spirit.

Say I have a dear friend and ask of him a gift to serve as a reminder of him, and he gives me a napkin. "Oh my, what a napkin; it was given me by a bishop!" Or, "This cloth belonged to Abba Abraam![8] I'll keep it in a box and decorate it on the outside." What do you think, then, if this Bible came down from God's own bosom? You would care for it as you would care for God's bosom. Believe me, if your nose were sensitive to spiritual things, it would sense God's own breath (*nefess*). This "breath" is the Holy Spirit, for "spirit" in Hebrew is *ruuah* or *nefass. Nefass kodush* (Holy Spirit) is the Hebrew—*Ruuah kodush* or *nefass kodush.*

"And He breathed in them the breath of life."[9] Where did this breath go? Did it leave us? Careful! It can never depart. The breath of God is within you! Can you sense it with me? But still you aren't able to imagine it. Believe me, if you sat alone and reviewed the words Father Matta told you, you would say to God, "I want to discuss these

8 Renowned twentieth-century saint who lived in upper Egypt.
9 Gen 2:7

things just between You and me. Can I really sense You within me? Can I smell You with my spirit?" For he said "breath," and the original language says the same: "He *breathed* . . ." So Your breath, O Lord, is in me—Your Spirit is in me! Then I cannot live any longer if I do not feel You in me. How can Your breath and Spirit be in me, and I not sense You?

Ah, O Lord, this morning Your Bible is before me. My Lord, if this Book had not been written, and we wished to have authentic words come down from You, what a price we would pay! How much would we toil just to hear a sentence proceed from Your mouth! And this whole Bible is sent from You by the Holy Spirit. I own it, but I am too slothful to sit every day to read for just fifteen minutes to half an hour! The Bible is God's special gift—from His Spirit, from Himself—given to me. The least I can do is to honor the Bible by devoting to it the best time of the day. The first fruits of my life! My youth, O Lord, I consecrate to You and to Your lovely Bible. Every morning I direct my eyes to Your Bible to enjoy it.

Ah, when I entered monasticism thirty years ago, the world had me busy with much work, learning, and studies, so I forgot the skill of reading and my mind was adverse to it. So I told my mind, "Oh, no, my friend, did we come to the desert to sleep?" Never! I don't ever want to read half a chapter and find my mind rusted and unable to read, and I begin to yawn like that yawning monk. I said, "No, Lord, this isn't my work—never! I *must* change myself by any means." So I began to stay up late. And of course my lamp was dim, and I let it burn low so that the oil might last. So I said to Him, "O Lord, give me grace!" And I prayed abundantly, until the Bible opened up before me, and I began to comprehend it richly. I found the light and glory of the Gospel to be an extraordinary thing.

Then I was struck with terror, and I began to feel a gloomy sadness. After the Bible had opened to me, after I felt its power and authority over myself and my life, and after I felt the power of the change that came over my mind and heart—in a remarkable fashion day by day—I began to sorrow and grieve, and I began to weep prodigiously. Why? I said, "O Lord, Your Bible is overabundant with good things. From just a few verses, I received a bounty of goodness. When will I finish all these epistles? When will I finish all these Gospels? When will I finish the Old and New Testaments? Lord, at this rate, I need at least one or two hundred years. I have a young, attentive mind, and You know that it won't stay with me long." And I wept much.

I put down the Bible and said, "My Master, You must give me either of two things. The first is to grant me long life and a youthful mind in order to comprehend the entire Bible—for what a shame that I've known You these thirty years, and I have only another ten or twelve before my mind shuts down. No, Lord. Right now, covenant with me to grant me a sharp mind and youth that I might live long enough to comprehend the whole Bible. Or grant me an extraordinary comprehension, by which I would be compensated for all these lost years. Let a month of my life be equal to a year or two in understanding. Otherwise, Lord, I won't be able to read and will remain very sorrowful. I want to understand, and I want to rejoice. I fear a lack of understanding, and that my life might pass by without finishing the Bible in all its beauty!"

And I meditated upon the entire Bible—Old and New Testaments—and became contented and satisfied to the fullest extent. It's the source of blessing in my life, and the source of my consolation, my support, my light and salvation, and every word in it is a joy to me. I open it anywhere and find light before me. When I am weary, I open and find rest.

"Paul, a bondservant of Jesus Christ, called *to be* an apostle, separated to the gospel of God, which He promised before through His prophets in the Holy Scriptures." The meaning of the verse reaches its fullest in the query God here poses: Was My Son prophesied of in the Bible? For what is the Bible about, and the promise, but about My Son—who came from the seed of David according to the flesh. O Son of God, Your entire Bible, including Your sonship in the entire Old Testament, revolves around the work You accomplished—around the incarnation accomplished through the Virgin Mary, who herself was of the house of David. All the Bible, including all the Old Testament, tells the story of Your sonship—which was before all ages. It was a hidden reality, unknown to humanity beforehand, but was proclaimed in these last days by the prophets and apostles.[10] This sonship which was veiled before all ages was proclaimed and made known, my Lord, on the day of Resurrection, by the Holy Spirit who taught it to Your disciples.

O Son of God, the desire of my heart is that You would make me able to fathom You, to know You, and to feel You, in both Your humanity and Your divinity. Every person we know, my Lord, has a fleshly lineage—father and grandfather—by which we may explore his character inherited through the flesh. As for You, O Son of God, You inherited everything from the Father! So grant me to fathom You, not as One who merely inherited a body, but as He who bears my own body. And teach me Your divine qualities which You delivered to us through the Holy Spirit.

You all know that Christ is the "King of kings." He is not just a king, but the King of kings, because He was given authority over all of heaven and earth. From the standpoint of the kingship He inherited as the offspring of David, this is what He bequeathed to us in the flesh. So we as a church or congregation are, as it is said, kings and priests.[11] We shall reign with Him. From the standpoint of the priesthood, as you can see, there are priests in the Church. The priesthood of the

---

10   Heb 1:2
11   1 Pet 2:9

Church is also an inheritance, inherited by Christ for us, and given to us as a gift. So when Paul here says that He sprang from the seed of David according to the flesh, it was not for Christ's own sake.

O Lord, grant the present listeners a spiritual understanding and an open heart! Everything that was written was written for us. Everything that happened to Christ happened for us. Every word here is for me, O Son of God. So grant me my portion; here we read, and I wish to know what my portion is in these words.

"O Son of God, did You really come from the seed of David and take flesh from the Virgin to grant it to me? O my Lord, I must learn all my theology over again. Is your humanity really for me?"

"Yes."

"Well, then, it's not just a mere bit of theology to be memorized! The Incarnation is a gift—a gift in all its particulars specifically meant for me! Is the body You took from the Virgin, and the body the Virgin took from her mother (of the seed of David) bequeathed to me? Do You mean, Lord Jesus, that *I* am of the seed of David?"

"Yes."

"A mysterious thing! Do You mean that *I* am a son of Abraham without realizing it?" Notice the verse: "We are Your children, yet Abraham did not know us."[12]

"O Lord, am I really a son of Abraham?"

"Yes."

So are Your words to Abraham true, that "All the nations will be blessed through you"?[13] Yes, and I am one of those to whom Abraham's blessing has reached. For I am now, my brethren, of David's seed and of Abraham's seed.

This is a mysterious and wondrous thing! I am part of the Israel

---

12 This is not an exact quotation from the Bible, but it is probably derived from St. Paul's discussions on the relationship between Abraham and the Christian found in Rom 4 and Gal 3.

13 See Gen 18:18.

of God! So are we true Israelites, in whom is found no deceit?[14] Most truly. And the message is confirmed: Israel strayed, but we came and took up the right and straight path. Had it ever entered your mind that you are a son of Abraham? It's a difficult thought. Let us thank God for our session today and for the Apostle Paul's words.

"Born of the seed of David according to the flesh, and declared to be the Son of God with power according to the Spirit of holiness, by the resurrection from the dead." O Lord, I have an even greater portion in this! My mind has begun to open up—give to them [the listeners] and to me, O Son of God!

He was declared Son of God on the day of the Resurrection. People said, "We thought he was a mighty prophet, but sadly he turned out to be no prophet. They seized him and subjected him to a violent death on the Cross. We thought He would come down from the Cross to reveal His power, but He wasn't able."[15] Who said these things?—the disciples! They lost all hope and sat dejected in a dark room to escape the notice of the Jews. They were in grief and sorrow because Christ had been three days in the tomb; and the Jews sought to ruin them.

Then came the ring of joy, "Christ is risen!" Risen? Yes! It's not possible! It's His spirit! Then Christ went to them Himself and said, "The words you spoke on the road were false. Do you now say among yourselves, 'It's His spirit'? Come, touch, what do you feel?"

"Your hand, Lord!"

He told them, "A hand has flesh and bones. Now put your finger in the nail prints."

They did. "Now, where's Thomas?"

"Here I am."

"Thomas, they say you won't believe until you place your fingers in the nail prints? Give me your finger."

---

14   See John 1:47.
15   See Luke 24:19–21.

He placed his fingers and cried out, "My Lord and my God!"

Faith began to appear in them. Then on Pentecost, the Holy Spirit came and revealed all the spiritual depths, and they knew that this is the Son of God.

But I desire, O Jesus, that You search my heart more, that I might better know the height and breadth of my sonship. For I tend to consider, Lord, that I obtained my sonship by my sweat and toil; but it is now clear that Your Body has been given me completely and freely. I do not pay a fee to the priest when I take Communion. I say, "What is this you're giving me?"

He answers, "The Body of Christ."

I ask, "Is it a piece of Him, like a finger?"

He responds, "No, it is the entire Body."

I say, "What? Forgive me, Father, and pray accept my foolish ignorance; but do I really partake of all of Christ—*all of Him?*"

"Yes."

"You mean this is *all* of Christ in the flesh?"

"Yes."

"My God! How then can I place Him inside me?"

"You still haven't understood, my son. Know that your hands are now Christ's hands, your feet Christ's feet, your eyes Christ's eyes."

"*Abouna,*[16] I have more to say: my members are not clean."

"Did you not hear Paul, 'Shall I take the members of Christ and make them members of a harlot?'"[17]

"Ah, my Lord, are my members really not mine?"

"Yes, for you took Christ's complete body. You are now His hands and feet."

Have you ever seen a good priest serving in the Spirit and converting

---

16 A colloquial Arabic term used to address the priest, simply meaning "father."

17 1 Cor 6:15

hundreds? What would you say of him? You would say, "These are Christ's hands," or "This is the mouth of the Holy Spirit." Every person in whom the Holy Spirit dwells and whose temple He purifies—"you are all pure by the words I have spoken to you"[18]—is filled with Christ.

St. Paul says, "But we have the mind of Christ."[19] Ah, even Christ's mind becomes my mind! Have you ever seen someone calm and meek, who displays the mind of Christ when he speaks? We are all called to have this mind of Christ. We are all called to possess the members of Christ; and we are all called to glorify Christ in our body—which is God's.[20] You are wholly owned by God, because Christ and the Holy Spirit dwell in you. You see now how to read about Him who "was born of the seed of David according to the flesh"?

I thank You, my God, for this Christ is for me, in me, and with me forever. I thank You, Lord, that You are completely mine—all Your humanity and divinity. With all boldness I can stand and say, "Our Father who art in heaven . . ." If not for You, Jesus, I would not dare to say to Your heavenly Father, "my Abba." Don't we say in the Thanksgiving Prayer, "the Father of our Lord, God, and Savior Jesus Christ"? Why the emphasis? To show us that we were estranged from the Father, and the Father could not draw near to us; between us and Him was fixed an impassable gulf. But Christ came and closed the gulf. He took our body, as Son of God, and united us with Him.

Ah, Son of God, many good things await us. Do you now know Jesus Christ our Lord? *Jesus* is the human name given by the angel, and *Christ* is the title of His priesthood as the Anointed of God. Even His very name He gave to us, because we have all become "Christians" and "anointed." The Roman Catholics have even boldly appropriated the name *Jesus* for their order, the Jesuits. *Jesus*-ians—they did not

---

18 John 15:3
19 1 Cor 2:16
20 1 Cor 6:20

even leave out His personal name! We took His sonship, we took His title, we took His personal name, Jesus: there is nothing left that is only His. Can you name me something He kept for Himself? Nothing, nothing at all! Oh, for the generosity of Jesus! Our Lord Jesus Christ—to Lord we add Master, and sole Savior. "Through Him we have received grace and apostleship for obedience to the faith among all nations for His name."[21]

I will now recap the method of reading: I read a verse and meditated, then joined it to the following verse to produce a deeper understanding; and after every reading followed a prayer. Is what I did today difficult? I did not say anything hard; all is quite simple. We started with *Paul*, then *bondservants*, then *called*, then *apostle*. Believe me, if you bring me the most profound commentary on the epistle, you will not find in it anything more than what you have just heard. Bring me Chrysostom, or Augustine the philosopher, or any expository book, and you will find that we were able to comprehend more. I did not do anything new; anyone can do what I did—to seize upon every verse and find what it has in store for him. And we discovered every word has something for us. *Bondservant, called, apostle, separated,* and the rest each contained something for us and is ours. What then? Is the entire Bible ours? Yes. And since it is ours, the Spirit is ready to explain it to you. The entire Bible and all its verses were preserved until this day to reach you as a pledge from heaven.

You can stand before God and quarrel with Him, "Look, either grant me to live this verse or erase it from the Bible. For whom have You written it? The saints? If so, they are splendid and do not need it; but I am lowly and weak, and these verses apply to me. Lord, I see it as my right to request this. I want to read and not lose one verse. I beseech You, who opened the apostles' minds, to open my mind. This is my foundation; what else could be? Could I establish my faith on

21 Rom 1:5

Matthew Henry or Chrysostom? Lord, I am living in *this* generation, my throat is parched, and I desire something to satisfy my heart. I desire words to speak to *me*. You opened the minds of the disciples, so You have this power, and it is not difficult for You. Open my mind, and show me what is my portion in my Bible."

How long did it take us? One hour—to reach verse 5. We agreed initially that it is a marvelous thing to read a chapter in an hour. It turned out that five verses took an hour, but what an hour! Believe me, when you read these words you will find many prayers on the way. When you stand before God boldly, God cannot bear it; He grows weak before the sinner and is overcome. As for the righteous, they will never receive mercy. But when the sinner weeps and says, "I am frail," God will help Him. "Lest by his continual coming he weary Me"— hear what the unjust judge said.[22]

Your heavenly Father attends to those who cry out to Him night and day.[23] Do you want to learn how to cry out? I have just shown you how. Believe me, if you are willing to start at seven o'clock in the evening, without having duties to busy you, and even to put off supper if needed, and to sit with God and read His Word at length without looking at the clock, you will find yourself up until morning. "O Lord, I've been up seven hours reading and praying without feeling the time pass!" All your reading will be turned to prayer and crying out to God. "My Lord"—"Do not forsake me"—"Grant me this"—He desires to hear these things. You *will not* receive from God if you do not do so! I tried many times without this way, and I did not receive; but by this way I received very much.

The gifts of God await the man who stubbornly and persistently seeks to overcome God. "Lord, it's been so long since You gave me anything; I'm going to wait till morning for You to grant me some

---

22 See Luke 18:5.
23 Luke 18:7

good." You say this kneeling, reading, weeping, and entreating. "If I were good, Lord, then You would not need to grant me anything. But I am weak; and if You leave me like this, I will become a wanderer in the streets. And after several years, the church servant will visit me no longer at home but in the bar. Lord, I am weak, and the adversaries are many. So I beseech You, strengthen me in Your Word, for You will not find anyone weaker than I. I am in need of spiritual fervor to fill me and preserve me in this evil world. I wait for You now. I have come on my own two feet, without anyone having visited me. I cry out to You, without anyone having taught me. Do not leave me alone. For I heard that You will never leave anyone empty. So here I cry to You, that You fill me and comfort me and strengthen me. Amen!"

All You have heard from me now, O Master, may it be the cry of us all, that You might hear from heaven all supplicants, that their hearts be opened to the Word of life, and learn of the Spirit as He is and not merely what is said of Him. The fiery Spirit, who dwells within and teaches all that Christ gives Him—all the mysteries of the Cross, suffering, death, and resurrection. Yes, O Spirit of God, who taught the saints, and rendered them full of knowledge and not just teachers of knowledge, and who taught the whole world, grant us now to live by the word of salvation, to be fortified by the Bible, and open our minds, that we be illumined by God's light. O Son of God, though we are weak and unworthy children, through the intercession of Your saints, make us truly worthy to be called children of the saints. Amen. O Lord, hear us and answer our prayers. Amen.

PART IV

On Feasts and Fasts

Hail to You, O Cross!

FEAST OF THE CROSS, 1976

"Hail to the Cross! Hail to the life-giving Wood!"[1] A strong objection arises in the mind of each of us at times which asks, "How can we say, 'Hail to the Cross'? Is the Cross a person? How can I be so materialistic as to say, 'Hail to the wood of the Cross'? Do we worship idols, as the Protestants say of us?" But in truth, we thank God for the Cross of our Lord Jesus Christ, and for that marvelous Wood, upon which were proclaimed the inner mercies hidden before all ages in the Father's bosom.

I was speaking with some of the abbas about the disciples who followed the Lord, how they didn't realize they were following God. They rather liked Christ because He was a healer and a feeder. "Ah, we will never hunger or thirst again!" they said. Then followed that strange act when the people attempted to raise Him up to make Him a king.[2] At least they saw in the healings and signs an indication that

---

1   Coptic doxology of the Feast of the Cross
2   John 6:15

He would lead Israel to an earthly salvation. They felt their situation with Him to be better than that of the Israelites in the wilderness with the manna; and Christ saw this as a kind of gain. It was a measure of truth. And then the mother of James and John asked of Christ, "Grant my sons to sit one on your right and one on your left in the kingdom."[3] But she meant a kingdom that would appear on earth, a type of Davidic kingdom, without any thought of death or eternal life. All minds were centered on an earthly reign!

This manner of materialistic thinking and earthly ambition were not overcome until the Cross. Oh, hail to the Cross! It overthrows every type of ambition and aim at worldly profit. The day a person begins to feel he is something important in the world is the day the Lord reminds him of the Cross; and he immediately forgets all his false hopes and clings to it. Hail to the Cross, which is capable of cleansing our thoughts and consciences from every earthly hope and temporal aim!

When the Cross first made its appearance, Peter, who considered himself "prime minister" of the disciples, fled. He stood watching from afar; then John (as I imagine it) asked him, "Would you like me to speak to the high priest for you?"

He said, "No, no, I'd rather follow events from a distance. You go inside." So he just stood outside with the servants—but they exposed him.

See how grace pursues the believer! Hide under a different name, and the name gets exposed; hide behind a mask, and the mask is exposed; hide behind dishonest talk, and the talk is exposed. Grace pursues us to the very end. For when God loves a person, He chastens him.[4]

Hail to the Cross, for it brought an end to all the false bonds that tied the disciples to the Lord. As we said, the Cross exposes every false

3   Matt 20:21
4   Heb 12:6

ambition, just as it abolished the disciples' aims when they all fled. Christ had told them, "This night you will all leave Me, but I am not alone."[5]

Blessed is the Cross, which reveals every pretense of the heart, the conscience, and the tongue! "Though all the disciples forsake You, I will never forsake You"[6]—thanks be to the Cross, O Peter, for it brought an end to this false pretense and false supremacy!

How often I see this in people who say to me, "O Abba, because of what you've done for me, I will support you until the day of my death!"

At that moment I laugh inside and think to myself, "Crucify Him, crucify Him."[7]

In truth, my beloved, our discussion on the Cross can extend to considerable length, and I don't know if you or I have the energy to last long enough; but let us continue our vigil. The mystery of the Father, the mystery of love, was hidden from all ages before the Cross. The promises of the Father to man were consistently doubted—as His promise to Abraham that he would have a son[8]—for man was incapable of feeling the Father's love. The love, the faithfulness, and the promises of the Father cannot be revealed to man just by word or thought; there must be tangible proof. Christ Himself came, the very image of the Father, and the icon of His essence—but neither then did man believe. He told them, "If you do not believe My words, then believe for the sake of the works";[9] but they believed neither words nor works.

The tragic events surrounding the Cross caused every last hope Christ could have had in man to be extinguished. Even the disciples of Emmaus told with sorrow of their failed hopes in the One they

---

5   John 16:32
6   Mark 14:29
7   Luke 23:21
8   Gen 17:19
9   John 14:11

thought was the Savior.[10] But on the day of the Resurrection, the truth of the Cross was declared; and the Holy Spirit came on the Day of Pentecost and threw light on all the works of Christ. They saw the Cross as the revelation of the Father's compassion. It needed neither wisdom nor philosophy. They proclaimed that Cross on which the Lord of glory was crucified, and people responded, "Does the Father love us so much that He would give His only Son?" Yes!

The Cross made all of God's doings a touchable reality, whereas wonders, contemplation, and philosophy are all impotent in comparison. St. Paul said that the Cross was considered foolishness to the Greeks and a stumbling block to the Jews, but to us it is *power*.[11] Tell me, then, is this a "contemplative" power? Can the power of God be a mere thought? A philosophy? What is *power*, Abbas? Power is an *active* or *working energy*. Electricity is an active energy; light is an active energy; wind is an active energy. Every type of power is an energy *at work*. And now—would you believe it—our spiritual life has entered into this realm of power! Spirituality has become *dunamis*[12] for human life, an energy that can do things. Remember how Christ healed the bedridden man by just saying, "Get up"[13]—how is that for working energy!

The Cross of our Lord Jesus Christ has entered into human life as a touchable reality and as a working, acting energy and power. Don't I have the right then to say, "Hail to the wood of the Cross"? I don't mean the literal wood of the Cross; for even if you brought that to me today, it wouldn't raise anyone from the dead.

"How can you say that, Abba?" you'll respond.

Let me tell you. Which is greater, the wood or Christ Himself?

---

10 Luke 24:13
11 1 Cor 1:23
12 Greek word for "power," from which are derived the English terms *dynamite, dynamic, dynamo,* etc.
13 Matt 9:6

"Christ," you say. Well, Christ was not able to perform signs in Capernaum.[14] Can you explain to me the meaning of "was not able"? I don't want to analyze the meaning too minutely, to avoid offending sensitive consciences. But the mind stalls at such words; they will vex and fatigue your brain. But He was not able to perform signs in Capernaum—which means He tried. Did He try or not? And was He able or not? Do not respond. Now that was Christ. So neither is the wood of the Cross able, of itself, to effect anything. But what is able?

"Do you believe that I am able to heal you?"[15]

"Yes, Lord!" and they worshipped Him. So when I say, "Hail to the wood of the Cross," I'm expressing my *faith* in this wood, upon which was crucified—my goodness!—the Son of God.

The Church's hymn of salvation is expressed in the Song of Songs, a book which carnal man will never understand. The Fathers used to forbid any person with an impure mind from hearing a sermon on the Song of Songs. When Gregory of Nyssa would come to speak on this book, he would say, "All you unstable youth, who have not yet been confirmed in purity and love, depart! These words are not for you." He wanted no one with a mind distorted by the world to stumble.

So today, when we say, "Hail to the life-giving wood of the Cross," I ask (forgive me) all the Protestants to depart, along with all such who look unfavorably upon our Orthodox worship.[16] We express our worship in words and hymns that are indiscernible to anyone not steeped in the depths of divine mystery. So we refuse to surrender for an hour, not even for ten minutes, to those who enter in to spy on our freedom in Christ Jesus.[17] The divine *love*, hidden from all ages, hidden

---

14 Mark 6:5

15 Matt 9:28

16 In the audio, this phrase is spoken very light-heartedly, with a modest chuckle from the great Abba, who never harbored a trace of ill-will or resentment toward any person in another denomination or church.

17 Gal 2:4

from the great and wise, was nailed to the wood. How wonderful—give me that wood!

"Here, take this piece, which has been preserved for almost two thousand years."

No! My friend, I speak about the wood in the mystical sense. I praise that wood in a spiritual, exalted sense.

I wish for the Cross to be held before my eyes from the dawn of my youth till the dusk of my old age, that I might meditate on it every day as it bears the Blood. No passing of time can erase it from my mind; no hand can lift it from my sight; no thief can steal it from me. Other religious relics can be stolen; they stole the head of St. Mark and sold it from place to place for years, as you all know the story. But I don't want what thieves can take. I desire a treasure that can neither be stolen nor decay.

The base of the Cross is planted on earth *and* in my heart. How both, you ask? I don't know; but so it is. Its base is on earth (and in my heart), while its height touches heaven; and upon it hangs the Son of Man, as the angels of God ascend and descend upon Him.[18] In this wood I see my salvation, my sanctification, and my righteousness, which I would not have been able to achieve by my own arm, nor by the arm of a prophet or even an angel. I embrace this wood in my soul during my troubles, my injustices, and my tears; and I find incredible comfort.

Hail to the wood that purges me from every thought that is not pleasing to Your goodness! Hail to the wood that fortifies me against every assault of the enemy, whether by wrong thoughts, by jealousy, by pride, by forgetfulness, by anxiety, by laziness, or by the decay of a bad life. Hail to the life-giving Cross, which if I enter the eternal sleep, will be to me not a grave but wings, by which I will soar. Hail to

---

18 John 1:50

the wood that is a rod and staff[19] to help me along my way, even when every person has forsaken me and I have nothing left in the world, until I reach life's end and arrive at the open door of heaven, bearing the Cross of our Lord Jesus Christ. Such, my beloved, is the doxology of the Church on the day she sings "Hosanna!"[20] If only the song of the Feast of the Cross would become the song of our entire lives! As you go and come, and move here and there, say, "Hail to the life-giving Cross!" O Cross of the Lord Jesus, grant me the Lord's peace!

The Bible says, "And He went out bearing His cross to the place called 'Place of a Skull.'"[21] *Bearing His cross.* Think of the Lord's words, "He who does not take up his cross cannot be My disciple."[22]

"Lord, is my cross other than Yours?"

"Yes, My son, I have My Cross and you have your cross."

What's the difference? I'll tell you. The Lord's own self was crucified upon His Cross. An astonishing miracle! Even if we sat here till morning, even if my brain could organize every thought, I still couldn't express the miracle.

It was impossible that Christ bear the condemnation of sinful man unless He first *emptied Himself.* Even before He came down to earth, He subjected Himself to a very strange and incredible self-emptying; for God could not take unto Himself a body from the earth's dust, and unite eternally with such a weak element, without self-emptying. For absolute weakness to unite with absolute strength is an event incomprehensible to the mind—but it occurred by an ability in God's nature unknown to man. We may say that in God's nature there is an attribute called "self-emptying," by which He can take unto Himself

---

19 Ps 23:4
20 Abba Matta refers here to the Feast of the Cross, in which the "Hosanna Tune" is used to chant the church hymns. The context does not seem to refer specifically to Palm Sunday.
21 See Matt 27:33.
22 See Matt 10:38.

something completely incompatible with His honor and power. He took a part of His creation and made it a part of Himself. Now, this divine attribute is not found in us; but in His mercy He placed in us an image or reflection of it. He gave us the ability to partake of a divine attribute called *humility*. We call it "humility," but in actuality it's the act of self-emptying.

Christ emptied Himself in order to be incarnate and in order to be crucified. But to be crucified meant that He made no claim to "self." This was made very clear during His trial. He didn't defend Himself; for if He had defended Himself, He would not have been crucified. His refusal to defend Himself was an integral part of the Cross. Thus He acted before Pilate, Herod, and Caiaphas. With one word He could have shaken up and repelled His judges and adversaries. Paul, on the contrary, appealed to Caesar; but they still executed him. The appeal[23] was simply a hidden intention of the Holy Spirit to allow Paul to carry the Gospel to the household of Caesar. But to bring one's case before Caesar is a lost cause—what can Caesar do for you? They said to Christ, "Defend Yourself!" but He wouldn't, because then He would not have been crucified. So the self-emptying that occurred at the Incarnation was revealed also at the Cross, but in a violent way. He endured the violence of slaps, insults, spitting in the face, strikes to the head, thirty-nine lashes, and blood falling everywhere—but never did He speak.

Let me give you a kind of strange analogy, Abbas. Imagine I'm walking toward you from afar, and a rough worker comes up to me, deals me a couple of fierce blows, and I fall to the ground. He hits me so hard in the stomach that my organs come out, and I writhe in pain on the ground; but none of you can come near me. Then he hits me in the head with his boot and breaks it. What would be your feelings? Even if you happen not to like me, imagine this happening to someone

---

23 Acts 25:11

you love. Imagine this happening to a beloved family member, while he opens not his mouth; and the perpetrator is even a weakling, a young boy. You would say, "Why isn't Abba doing anything? Why doesn't he hit him back? Abba is strong, but this kid is weak; he can knock the kid out with a single hit! Abba, do something!" But the kid keeps hitting me till he exposes my organs and steps on my neck and kills me.

The Cross is nothing less, Abbas! What heroism, O Jesus, what greatness, O God! It twists and confounds the mind! This can make one go mad thinking about it! If a human saint had done this, we would make statues of gold and write thousands of poems about him. Consider Joan of Arc, who just for leading an army had statues made of her and poems written about her. Consider the saintly monk Bonaventura, and all the poetry and acclamation he received for being burned alive while confined in prison. The saints give us a small picture of the Cross, but Christ is the ultimate hero.

When Christ died on the Cross, He paid the price for all those who died and who would die. Life itself died; and thus life was granted to all those who die in Christ Jesus. Death reached its end on the Cross. This was the Cross of our Lord Jesus Christ. We are blessed to receive and put on this Cross—without any pain or suffering on our part—by the Spirit in baptism. We are signed by the Cross, receiving redemption, and salvation, and righteousness, and eternal life.

One may ask, "Is there a price that I pay for this Cross?"

"None."

"Any labor or work?"

"No."

"So the Cross that caused our Lord violence and abuse is given me for free?"

"Yes, freely."

"And His death is given freely?"

"Yes, freely."

Freely! By the Cross the Father was pleased to reveal, from within the depths of His being, the fullness of His love toward all generations; it was a sacrifice given for humanity, that we might receive the sonship and divine image through Christ Jesus. All who have been baptized have put on Christ; this "putting on" means receiving His complete image—in death and resurrection. This gives us, therefore, the image of the slaughtered Son before the Father; and thus we receive favor and acceptance. All these blessings are dependent upon the transferal of the Son's image to us. We are being transformed into the same image from glory to glory.[24]

Christ gave us this image and said, "Now I want you to carry your cross." What is our cross? I will explain it simply and briefly. Our cross is to suffer pain, and to sacrifice our lives, and to deny ourselves— for the sake of others. It is not for any advantage to yourself. All the advantages that accrue to *you* are derived from Christ's Cross. It's by Christ's Cross that you die to the world and the world to you.[25] All your lusts and desires, along with the flesh of the old man, are crucified, not on your cross, but on the Cross of Christ. The cross you carry on your back cannot forgive your sins or crucify you to the world. All such things—salvation, redemption, righteousness, and the death of the old man's desires—are accomplished by Christ's Cross. Then what is *my* cross? You cannot approach Christ, or be united with Him, or take His image, without bearing your cross. "Take up your cross and follow Me" means to be always ready to abandon the self for the sake of others.

Let's dwell upon this idea a while because it's not a small matter. We saw that Christ suffered beatings and pain, not for Himself, but for the sake of others. This is the cross we are called to bear in this

---

24 2 Cor 3:18
25 Gal 6:14

generation, in order to fill up the sufferings of Christ in our bodies.[26] My cross is not that I should suffer for myself, or endure trials for my own salvation. Would my enduring all injustice or persecution grant me salvation? Not at all—what saves me is Christ's Cross. But I accept injustice and persecution primarily for the sake of him who persecutes me and for the sake of my message to the world. Herein I take up the image of Christ and the Cross.

You might say, "This is a hard saying, Abba! You mean that if I don't endure the insults and attacks of people, I am deprived of the cross?"

"Yes."

"Then prove it by a verse."

Fortunately a verse just came to me now while I was speaking: "If you do not forgive men their trespasses, neither will your Father in heaven forgive your trespasses."[27] Imagine if the Father withheld forgiveness from me; would I then have salvation? Would I have anything in Christ's Cross? Nothing. I am deprived of the Cross if I refuse to forgive my brother. So the cross that I must bear is to sacrifice, to renounce myself, and to endure tribulations unto death, for the sake of my brother and for the world. A very strange and astounding thing!

Hail to the Cross, which by the mystery of Christ hidden in it is able to grant me endurance of pain for the sake of others! It teaches me to endure persecution with thanksgiving, to endure injustice and humiliation without defending myself.

"Abba Matta, they're saying such-and-such about you!"

I can only respond, "Hallelujah." What a bitter cross I once endured when they informed me of malicious things said against me! A bitter cross indeed; but I persisted in swallowing up the words until they finally passed through my system, and the conclusion was praise. I gained strength. I gained joy, health, and resilience from that cross.

---

26 Col 1:24
27 Mark 11:26

Hail—I am insistent on this point—*hail* to the wood of the life-giving Cross! From the Cross we may receive strength upon strength, by the mystery of Christ, who was able to pass over the abyss of death without complaining or defending Himself. This is *strength*, Abbas, when a human is accused and does not defend himself. It is *strength*, Abbas, when someone insults and mistreats you, and you remain silent while you are swallowing up all the words, until they pass and their effect dies.

Hail to the wood of the life-giving Cross! Hail to the unbreakable power that issues from the wood of insult and injury! This was the power planted on the earth on the day of Golgotha. And from that day till the end of time, that power enters in to comfort every soul grieving, sorrowing, and persecuted. May God make you a people who take pleasure in the Cross of our Lord Jesus Christ; a people who take pleasure in defending the poor and the victims of injustice. May God allow you to participate in that wondrous picture of a lamb led to the slaughter, with the knife placed at its throat while it is calm and silent. It is silent because its owner is the one slaughtering it; it trusts him, because he was the one who fed it. How incredible that we learn from lambs and sheep! O Lord, what is this amazing example that You have placed in animals for us? Can you believe that Christ was symbolized as a lamb led to the slaughter?[28] I myself have many times seen a lamb being prepared for slaughter: it exhibits the utmost calmness. You tie its legs, but it doesn't move; you place the knife, and it doesn't move. It *trusts* the person who is its owner, and feeder, and caretaker.

Ah, beloved, let us trust exceedingly that the One who shepherds us is the One who will "slaughter" us. It is not at all the work of our adversary; for as He said, "You would have no power at all against Me unless it had been given you from above."[29] The knife descends from

---

28 Is 53:7
29 John 19:11

above. The nails were driven by a heavenly hand, and the hammer was sanctioned by the Father, who permitted the Crucified One to be hung on the Cross. Man himself can never bring you to be slaughtered, or harm your reputation, or steal your rights, unless it be allowed from above. Step forward, therefore, and fear not, but accept the cross and the knife—just like your Lord.

"He who desires to be My disciple must take up his cross and follow Me."[30] And the disciple will be crucified every day. The bitter is very *bitter*; don't ever think that your cross is an easy matter. The cross has in it the sting of death. When once the cross passes, you might feel relief and say, "Oh, thank God it's past!" but the next one soon follows! The cross is not a pleasurable thing in the least; God knows, it has not a thousandth fraction of pleasure in it. A person only rejoices after he has survived his cross. Remember Christ, who pushed through moment by moment, being severely oppressed by sufferings, though He refused to murmur a single complaint until the very end, when He finally cried out with a loud voice and gave up the spirit. Man similarly remains oppressed by trials and suffering until they pass and he says, "Thank You, O God!"

I once underwent an extremely bitter experience. Someone once went abroad and, without an ounce of right, spread the most loathsome rumors about me. The blow dazed me; so I ran to my cell and cried out in the name of Jesus Christ. This saved me, because I was on the verge of losing myself and reacting in an irrecoverable way. I cried out to Christ from my cell in a tremendously loud voice; it was the cry of someone on the verge of death. I found divine aid come upon me the same moment. But I could not bear it long. I went out of my cell after five minutes looking like a dizzy, ill, injured man. I suffered from that blow for years. For years I suffered from the injury, until it partially subsided; but it never completely disappeared.

---

30   Matt 16:24

This is a new message for us, Abbas, a very new understanding, and if we seize it, we will advance incredibly. The Cross of Christ will be transfigured in us. Abundant power, full of blessing and grace, will come upon us; and that power will lift us above this world, above all its straits, griefs, and needs. We are in urgent need of God's power. And there is no way of obtaining this power except by entering into the mystery of Christ's Cross. *Let him take up his cross and follow Me.*

The Nativity of Our Lord

1974

As we're accustomed to doing every year, beloved, we will contemplate the meaning of this occasion, that we might *live* it. For this is really the intention of the Church and of Christ, that such occasions be for our lives. We celebrate the Nativity today, but our celebration is not a mere remembrance; we have gathered for prayer and for liturgy that we might meet with Christ in Bethlehem. What we need is to "feel" Christ today. We do not simply read the Nativity narrative as from a book, but rather we stand before a heavenly event. The angels are witnesses. God proclaimed something on Christmas Day which neither narrative nor history itself can fully contain.

The divine Birth, beloved, means the Incarnation; and the Incarnation means that God appeared in the flesh. History cannot contain God's appearance, and it cannot be reduced to a mere story for meditation. I say, God's appearance is an *event*, a divine and heavenly event; the Gospel does not record the "history" of the Lord Jesus' birth, but records rather a heavenly happening. The Nativity happened within the course of history, but it is also the end of all history; for many prophecies proclaimed that the Lord's birth would be the sign of the "fullness of time."[1] We constantly read in the prophets about the coming Day of the Lord,[2] in Greek called the *eschaton*, which was considered to be the end of time. Any time period which has reached its fullness point can be considered to be complete and finished.

Therefore, we can say that Christ's birth is *above time*; and so we cannot deal with it as just a record with historical details to be analyzed. No, our intention this evening is to make a *living entrance* into the story of Christ's birth, to place it before ourselves as a heavenly occurrence which never changes and never ends. Again, no matter how long or wide history becomes, it will never be able to encompass the story of the Nativity. The Nativity is eternal life itself that shone forth from Bethlehem and remains shining until the end of the ages. So my purpose in this discussion with you tonight is that we make a living and meaningful entry into Christ's birth, one that is above time and above history. Unfortunately, we've grown accustomed our whole lives to read the Nativity story as simply something that happened about two thousand years ago.

I said before that the Nativity means the Incarnation, and the Incarnation is now the source of our lives. These words need explanation. As we read in John's Gospel, Christ was incarnate, the Word took flesh, and God appeared in a body. The Incarnation has become our lives, and it is the foundation of our Christian faith.

"Are you a Christian?"

"Yes, I am a Christian."

"Then what does it mean to be a Christian?"

"It means I believe in Christ."

"And who is He?"

---

1   Gal 4:4
2   Zeph 1:14, Joel 3:14, etc.

"Christ is God manifest in the flesh."

The Incarnation is the content of our lives, our faith, our doctrine, and the salvation we live every day. That is why I say that the Incarnation is not a mere story but rather life itself. It is also the hope we have that mends every weakness of man, and the brokenness of history, and every care and tribulation. The world with all its troubles has become as nothing in the light of the Incarnation, for it provides another and better life for man; for we will not be able to arrive at the truth and meaning of the Nativity while worldly issues and cares occupy our minds. This is what I wish for and ask God for: that all of us sitting in this church today would forget the world, forget time and history, forget our past with all its faults, frailty, and anxiety, and enter together into this divine event.

As we sit here together, I would like to imagine that our gathering is in Bethlehem. And our imagining is not fantasy, but very truth. Our question now is, what is our position or place in Bethlehem? Is it that of the Magi, who bore gifts from a far country, being led by the star, rejoicing that they would meet Christ and worship Him? They had indeed a lofty and wonderful role: to be a people who traveled a far distance to meet the king of the Jews and offer him the finest gifts they had. As we were taught from childhood, their gold, frankincense, and myrrh pointed to each of Christ's roles: as King, Prophet, and Suffering God. But I tell you, our position in Bethlehem is much greater than that of the Magi.

How about the shepherds, to whom the angel announced, "Rejoice with great joy, for there is born to you today in the city of David a Savior. Go, and this will be the sign to you: You will find a baby wrapped in swaddling clothes and lying in a manger."[3] They went happily and saw Him, and were filled with exceeding joy. So are we in the position of the shepherds? No again. Well then, let's go higher

---

3   Luke 2:10–12, quoted from memory.

and ask about Joseph. That righteous and just man, guardian of the Virgin Birth and faithful minister to the miraculous event—are we in his place? Again I will dare to say, no, but even higher.

Please do not take offense and say, "Abba, you've gone too far!" When I reach the end, you will realize that I did not go too far.

"Then what do you want to say?"

"Well, I want to come near the Virgin as well and ask, is our position in Christ like that of the Virgin Mother?"

"And your response?"

"I say, no again. Higher!"

"Higher than the Virgin? Now this is too daring!" But allow me to continue, because it is not my own teaching.

Judge for yourselves and understand our place in the Bethlehem stable from this: *We are bone of His bones, and flesh of His flesh.* We are Christ's own Body! If you want to verify my words, read St. Paul's words in the fifth chapter of Ephesians.[4] Joseph, as I said, is the guardian of the Virgin Birth, and Mary, the pure saint, is Mother; but you and I are His own flesh and bones! We comprise His entire Body. Therefore, I say, we are meeting with Christ in Bethlehem today, but it is an incredible and marvelous rendezvous; and it requires us to constantly and repeatedly review ourselves as well as the Nativity story.

I think you all now understand the terrible weightiness of this issue, and that it deserves the long introduction I gave, where I urged you to enter the Nativity outside the bounds of mere story and not to treat it as something confined to Matthew 1 and Luke 2. But we will enter it on an exceedingly lofty plane, one that is unbounded by the limits of history and time. I, the reader, am not an outside observer; I am not a mere interpreter; I am not a mere beneficiary of Christmas—rather, I am *flesh of His flesh and bone of His bones.* You and I take up a central place in Bethlehem. This One who is born, the

---

4   Eph 5:30

wonderful Child, this magnificent gift from heaven, contains me as a vital part.

Thus, my initial remark proves true that Christmas is not about remembrance or a past event or even Gospel history; but it's the beginning of a living relationship with Christ, an impressive and momentous relationship—a relationship that is the basis of our existence or *being*. Consider this sentence: Christ is born, therefore I exist.[5] If Christ is not born, then wipe out my existence. One of the philosophers[6] once said, "I think, therefore I am." He was one of those who wearied himself through intellectual speculation, but today I speak to you about real and life-giving things.

Christ's birth on that day was our eternal birth. Have you seen now what Bethlehem means to us? Existence, being, and eternal life— not just memory, ritual, or hymn. The hymn *"Pi-jen-misi"*[7] was not even chanted today; or maybe Abba Kyrillos sang a part of it, but we understood not a thing, and he neglected to even inform us of its meaning in Arabic. Thus are hymns and rituals performed in vain. Hymnology and ritual are important, of course; but if they do not take us to the higher vision and to the profound relation that binds us to Christ, then it is all for nothing. Otherwise, we just come, and sermonize, and sing, and have a merry time, then go to eat meat. If that's what the feast amounts to, then count me out. But the feast to which I invite you all this evening is the immediate entrance into the truth which the Nativity reveals for life and existence. Cancel Christmas, then cancel me too. If there is no Bethlehem, then there is no me.

As for Bethlehem itself, I don't believe I'm exaggerating when I say that it is really *our* origin of birth. Let me explain. Is Christ not the

---

5   A play on the Arabic words "born" (*mawlood*) and "exist" (*mawgood*).
6   René Descartes.
7   Famous Coptic hymn said during the Feast of the Nativity. A rough translation would be, "The virginal birth and spiritual pains: marvelous wonders, according to the prophetic sayings."

Head of the Church? Then if Christ was born in Bethlehem, is not Bethlehem our origin of birth?

If you ask me what country I'm from, I respond, from Bethlehem.

You say, "No, where were you born?"

I answer, "Bethlehem."

You reply, "What took you all the way over there?"

I say that I didn't go there, but Bethlehem came to me. It entered deep inside me, and I draw my existence from it. If the Garden of Eden of old was the origin of Adam's birth, where he fell into sin and was exiled, then Bethlehem is the new Eden; and we enter it never to leave again. It is our Garden, our heavenly Paradise, in which we shall live and eat of the tree of life forever, and never die.

My beloved, if we do not receive what is given to us by the sacred history in the correct spirit—that is, in the way I have just explained—then the Gospel was written in vain. We are in great need of reviewing the manner in which we read the entire Bible (not just the Nativity story), and I always present an example by which the Bible is to be interpreted on the mystical and spiritual plane. After you've received this key of interpretation, you will be able to open all the closed doors of Scripture; and you will delight in every line as a guide for your life.

How many times have we read the Nativity story together, and we've always harbored the idea that it was an incident exterior to us, something that happened a long, long time ago, in a Judean city. And in that time long, long ago, there were shepherds who received the announcement from heaven; and great joy was given them (though perhaps not to us), and they went to see the Child. Just a "story." Then from this story we begin fabricating phony toys. We go and make a manger out of cardboard paper; we decorate it with shimmering lights; we spend tons of money on the project, and act chirpy and jolly for the fanciful scene. But the truth is thus expelled from the story.

For the real manger, which sat on dirt to show me my nature, and the coarse and abrasive hay placed therein to show exactly on what level Christ accepted to meet with us—we go and overturn all this to make a fake manger and a plastic Jesus with which to amuse the kids. A fraudulent state of mind! A thinking foreign to the Gospel truth! This must never be the method of our encounter with the Bible. But today, we learn together a different method of encounter that ought to ever be our approach to Bible reading. It is to ask the question, "What is the relationship between what I read and my life?" For how was the Bible written, as a letter that kills,[8] or as a life-giving spirit? I must enter the story by the Spirit, in order to find my place, my life, my salvation.

I wanted to go through the whole story with you on this higher level, but I found the matter quite demanding. I said, "Lord, will I be able to lengthen my discussion with the hearers, some of whom have traveled from a great distance, and perhaps are as tired and weary as my abject self, and it is near midnight—will I be able to delve with them into the great depths of the Christmas story?" It is not really possible; but it will suffice us to touch on just a few light points.

Matthew's Gospel begins with the genealogy of Jesus Christ. I sat once to contemplate the first verse, which I will share with you now; and I only wish we had the time to analyze the entire passage and to meditate on each character in it. St. Matthew writes, "The book of the genealogy of Jesus Christ, the son of David, the son of Abraham."[9] It takes me by surprise; it's quite a jump from David to Abraham! But why David, and why Abraham, and what does it have to do with me?

In truth, deep calls unto deep in meaning. "Son of David" is the title that Christ assumed. And the psalms that were read today all spoke about the *kingship* of the Messiah. We call Jesus the Christ, or the

---

8   2 Cor 3:6
9   Matt 1:1

Messiah, or the Anointed One, or the Anointed King.[10] So the epithet "Son of David" resounds in my life as something very significant! It proclaims Christ's kingship, which directly points to the Kingdom of God. For God's promise to David—that one of his seed would sit on his throne *forever*[11]—was a pointer to God's Kingdom, which would be inaugurated by the birth of the Christ. In Bethlehem, the Son of David was born, and the Kingdom was thus summarily announced.

You will notice that in Matthew, a Gospel full of wisdom, after introducing us to the Nativity with such momentous words—"son of David, son of Abraham"—he decides to speak about the magi, but not about the shepherds. Why? His focus is the *Son of David*, or the kingship. The driving force that inspired the magi's wisdom and spirit was the search for the One who was born King of the Jews. You see the spiritual and mystical theme that moves through the Gospel! It's a golden thread of light and beauty woven throughout each line and each chapter, which occasionally surfaces to show itself for a time before submerging again. He begins the first chapter with Christ, the Son of David, then in the second chapter he exhibits His kingship.

And here is found Abraham's relationship to Christ. Remember that the promises and blessings of Abraham were limited to the nation of Israel, until Christ came and shattered the barriers, and transmitted the blessings to the Gentiles—to us. So, when St. Matthew writes, "the Son of David, Son of Abraham," he is pointing directly to me and you; *you* have a portion in the blessing; *you* have entered the inheritance; *you* have become of the seed of Abraham! The promise to Abraham is very pertinent to us; it is the blessing of faith. "In your seed shall all the earth be blessed."[12] St. Paul makes it very clear that it is not

---

10 In Arabic—a Semitic language that has many phonetic affinities to Hebrew—the words for *Christ* (Meseeh), *Messiah* (Meseyeh), *and Anointed One* (Meseeh) are all extremely similar.

11 2 Sam 7:16

12 Gen 22:18

in his *seeds*—in other words, it is not through many descendants of Abraham that the nations will be blessed, but through Christ alone. He writes, "To Abraham and his Seed were the promises made. He does not say, 'And to seeds,' as of many, but as of one, 'And to your Seed,' who is Christ."[13] So, whenever the Gospel alludes to David, it emphasizes Christ's relationship to me as King; or the Kingdom which has been opened to me; or its opening inside of me—for the Kingdom is within us.[14] And when it alludes to Abraham, it speaks of the blessing and how it reached me through Christ's mediation.

St. Matthew said, "the Son of David, the Son of Abraham," then St. Luke continues with the words, "the son of Adam, the son of God."[15] Ah, how wonderful are these four steps in Christ's genealogy; and I would that the Spirit would give you a calm and peaceful hour, and a quiet spirit, apart from the cares of the world, and apart from any feelings of bodily want or human weakness, to enter the fullness of the grace of Christ, to enter the fullness of the Incarnation, and to contemplate together these four steps or stages: David, Abraham, Adam, and God. I have written about these four stages but won't be able to speak of them now; instead, I leave you the opportunity to meditate in the Spirit by yourselves upon each step, and to find the portion reserved for you in Christ. For, as I said before, the Gospel was written that we might believe that Christ is the Son of God, and that believing, we might have life in Him.[16]

Beloved, think with me upon old, wearied humanity, which is undone in its sin, which has squandered all its inheritance, even the beautiful image of God given to man at creation—where nothing was left for man except despair and wandering in the shadow of death. Mankind was, as it were, bound in chains, waiting for the dawn of

---

13 Gal 3:16
14 Luke 17:21
15 Luke 3:38
16 John 20:31

light. Then the Light appeared—but how did it appear? Did it shine on a screen? Did it appear as Noah's rainbow? Did it appear in the dream of any saint? *The divine Light of God appeared in my flesh and your flesh.* God met with humanity in this old, feeble flesh, which time had filled with anxiety, wants, and conflict. It is enough for anyone to read the Lamentations of Jeremiah to understand what I am saying. The long years of the past have filled man's soul with cries and wailing, which have swollen the pages of Scripture and have birthed the laments of the Psalms.

This came to an end, beloved, on the day of the Nativity. Bethlehem put an end to the sorrows of man. The past is done with, and the present is filled with heaven. God has appeared in the flesh, and it is the flesh of humanity. He took it *completely*, exactly as we have received it, with all of its emotions, sensitivities, feelings, weaknesses, with the single exception of sin. He took our flesh in order to reveal through it the abundance of His riches; He took it to display the abundance of His love. So our feast today, my beloved, is a feast of the restoration of that grand and lofty image in man, not just of the image with which Adam was created, but one much better indeed. In Hebrews, it says He is the "reflection of His glory, and the image of His essence."[17] The Lord Jesus bore our flesh and granted it the full honor of the Son of God. Beloved, this feast celebrates the restoration of mankind's honor and glory in Christ Jesus.

I say, we must enter this feast undefeated by our weaknesses; for if we enter overcome by them, we will not bask in the joy that was announced to the shepherds. Can the joy of heaven be arrested? Can sin choke it? Impossible. That is why I ask you, and beseech God, that we be able to enter the feast above our weaknesses, our anxieties, and the envy and enticement and decay of money. We must enter the Nativity surmounting all sin. All our hungers and sorrows must

---

17   Heb 1:1

be overcome, if even for only a moment, that we might receive our portion in the Nativity. We can regain our image in Christ. We can regain our glory and honor in Christ.

These are weighty words, and you might tell me, "Give me a verse I may lean against, because these things are too heavy for me." Listen to what the Apostle Paul says: "We all, with unveiled face, beholding as in a mirror the glory of the Lord, are being transformed into the same image from glory to glory."[18] I am not saying anything foreign to the Bible's message.

Let us go unto Bethlehem in order to meet the born One, to see Him with our eyes, to carry Him in our arms, to breathe in His scent, to gaze into His eyes, to inhale His breath. These meditations are perhaps more Syrian in nature and not as familiar to the Coptic Church. Anyhow, I am using them to take you into the truth, since other means are lacking. But I am not just going to take the Babe in my arms; I am not just going to inhale His breath. Rather, as I said before, Christ took my flesh: His breath is my breath; His scent has become my scent. How about if, instead of saying that humanity will regain its glory in Christ, I say that we will *see* (every day) and will *contemplate* (every morning and evening) the glory of Christ—that we might be changed into that image, from glory to glory.

Let me now speak to you as an individual, that my words might find a place in the heart of each one. My dear friend, if you feel that you have lost the best qualities of humanity—purity, holiness, trust, whatever it be—through weakness, ignorance, little faith, or low self-esteem (that foe of every generation)—I beseech you, my friend, to forget your entire past, even if it stings you until this hour—abandon it all this day and this very moment. For the sake of the One born in Bethlehem, come with me to meet Christ, who awaits you with open arms. Christ was not born to make a short visit on earth and then leave.

---

18   2 Cor 3:18

He was not a passing visitor. He was the Son of God, who took flesh, and who will never cast it off. He took *us*, beloved. He took humanity unto Himself and formed a union with it (a union keenly felt by the Orthodox Church), complete and perfect. All things that belonged to the divinity and humanity respectively are now united. What a wonderful doctrine! And this unity eradicated all the weaknesses of humanity without eradicating humanity itself or any of its traits.

Beloved, in the Spirit we assemble today in Bethlehem, in Adam's Paradise, the doors of which are opened to us never to be closed again. The cherubim no longer stand at the door with a flaming sword to prevent our entrance,[19] but they rather open their six wings to draw us into an intellectual and spiritual paradise. In Bethlehem God has revealed the deepest depths of His love and the deepest depths of His generosity to sinners, in order thereby to lift the burden of sin. We are no longer to live in the lamentations of Jeremiah, or the mourning of the Psalms, or the sorrows of Job, but in the joy of the shepherds, in an everlasting relationship with Christ.

O God of heaven, who announced from Bethlehem an eternal covenant, that sinful man might freely receive grace, unite us with Yourself this evening, that we might find joy and consolation in this Birth which is my birth, and in this new life which is given to us. Bless us, Lord, and may Your name be blessed in Your Church forever. Amen.

---

19   Gen 3:24

"I AM" in the Eucharist

HOLY THURSDAY, 1974

Human history is divided into two important eras or ages. The first age was represented by the books of the Old Testament. These spoke of a further "coming age," which would be inaugurated by the "day of the Lord"—the day of the Messiah. In the hearts of the Jewish sages, that day was yearned for as a turning point for humanity; and we are now living in it without realizing its significance.

This is really the theme of my discourse: how, by preserving our spiritual attentiveness, to realize the significance of this day. You will observe that the final verse in today's Gospel says, "But I say to you, I will not drink of this fruit of the vine from now on until that day when I drink it new with you in My Father's kingdom."[1] *From now until that day*—these words separate the old age, which desired salvation, from the coming age, "that day," the time of salvation. The key agent Christ used for this division of time was the Mystery of the Church, or the Mystery of Mysteries—that greatest mystery indeed

---

1 Matt 26:29

that humanity was ever given—the Sacrament of the Eucharist.

As we read, He took bread, broke, gave, and said, "Take, eat, this is My body." And He took the cup, gave thanks or blessed (for to "thank" and to "bless" are equivalent in Hebrew thought), gave, and said, "Take, drink, this is My blood." In these brief words He establishes the mystery that, as I said, embraces all other mysteries. But today I want to focus on three which are the most preeminent in our Christian lives.

The first I will call the Mystery of Christ, or the Mystery of "I AM." Christ used this expression, *ego eimi*, quite often. The Arabic translation of "I AM" is weaker than the Greek, which in turn is weaker than the Hebrew. The Hebrew contains the sense of "I AM He who exists in Myself," or "I AM the Self-existent," an existence dependent on nothing but the Self, without beginning or end. The Greek *ego eimi* reflects this meaning, but the Hebrew is deeper and stronger. So the question is, in the mystery of the Eucharist, in the broken Body and shed Blood, can we indeed find the idea of *ego eimi*, "I AM"—that is, Christ existing in Himself?

The second is the Mystery of the Body, which I will explain in its turn. The third is the Mystery of the Kingdom; and the question then is, do we find in this mystery the true proclamation of the Kingdom, or, in the words of the verse, a banquet of eating and drinking in the Kingdom?

I AM

Now, the first mystery, the "I AM": this phrase encompasses all that Christ had previously done and taught. He taught for three and one-half years; but what could He possibly do to prevent all that teaching from being lost? What could He have done to prevent the teaching from vanishing, not only from men's minds, but also from their active lives? For He said, "The words that I speak are spirit and life."[2] Could He entrust the words that contained such power of spirit and of life to the mere intellect of man? It would have failed to bear fruit!

The mind of man has always lacked the ability to raise itself from the level of earthly materialism to the height of mystical spirituality. Until today, the human mind confounds the very understanding of this mystery. If you only knew the number of books written, and the amount of controversy waged, and the mass of conflict raging between sects on the meaning of this mystery, you would be stunned! And why all this? Because men have approached the subject primarily with their human minds; and so schisms have naturally occurred, because human minds differ. The Western mind is different from the Eastern mind. And within Eastern thought, the Byzantine, Cappadocian, and Alexandrian minds are all different. So in order for Christ to unite human thought, to unite human action, to unify all His teaching—He inaugurated this mystery.

In brief, we want to explore how Christ transformed His teaching from mere intellectual theory to actual mystical life. When Christ says, "I AM," He gathers and summarizes the entire Gospel: I AM the Life; I AM Love; I AM the Light of the world; I AM the Way; I AM the Truth; I AM the Living Bread; I AM the True Vine; I AM with you until the end of the age; I AM coming quickly. In truth, brethren, when our Lord inaugurated this mystery, He infused in it every one of these I AMs! And through the mystery, He allows us to be raised from mere words to real active life. Let us now inquire how by this mystery He speaks to us the words, "I AM the Way," or Love, or Light?

The Gospel says, "When evening had come, He sat down with the twelve."[3] There was a supper involved here along with a love-feast. The love-feast, or *agape*, was observed with the eucharistic mystery

---

2   John 6:63
3   Matt 26:20

performed right in the center of it. The supper was held according to the rite of Palestinian Judaism, where two wine cups were offered: one at the beginning that bore no religious meaning, and one at the end that held very deep significance for the *agape*. It was called the "cup of blessing," which required all members to rise from the table and wash their hands before touching it. This is why you see the priest wash his hands before serving at the altar. So the Hebrew supper was immersed in spirituality, for it was also a love-feast.

By the end of the first century, all the churches of the world (save the Coptic) had separated the *agape* meal from the eucharistic mystery. After they had eaten and drunk, the broken bread and the cup would be offered separately as mystical elements. But in the Coptic Church, the eucharistic mystery continued to take its place in the middle of the *agape* meal, all the way up to the fifth century. We were even criticized by Western churchmen at the time for mixing the supper with the mystery; but that was the original rite! That was how Christ first presented His Body and Blood. It was a mystery of love, and Christ could not have offered it any other way. Tell me, what is the strongest expression of human love? Forgive me, but it's food; when a beloved guest comes to visit, you offer him the finest fare you have.

So, up until the end of the fifth century, the children of the Coptic Church would eat and drink and have a merry time, then consummate the feast with the mystery. Then some began to look at the churches in the West, in Byzantium and Palestine, and alarmingly declared the need to separate the supper from the mystery. These were church leaders who were beholden to Western thinking and so commenced the process of separation. But the cleavage did not happen immediately. They began by celebrating the mysteries first, then running to the tables to celebrate the *agape* meal together. And you will notice that in the churches of certain monasteries (such as those of Abba Pishoy, of the Syrians, and of Abba Antonios), the area located right before the

choir platform was the dining area. But then there came out a rule—
and why the author of it felt it necessary I don't know—"Eating inside
church is prohibited!" At that point they started divorcing the mystery
from love (*agape*).

What I want you to take away from this is the idea that a
congregation would assemble for the expression and exchange of *love*,
by way of the Body and Blood. Consider this verse, for example: "He
who loves his brother abides in light."[4] What we celebrate is a love-
feast, or in other words, a light-feast; and He who said, "I AM the
Light of the world," is present. You see now how the mystery of the
Eucharist includes the mystery of *ego eimi?*

Consider another verse: "He who hates his brother is a murderer."[5]
Whom does he murder? *Himself.* When I hate another, I am killing
myself. But then: "We have passed from death to *life* because we love the
brethren,"[6] and also, "I AM the life."[7] (Did you make the connection?)
So the *agape*, the love-feast, also involves *life*, because we have moved
from death to life. I AM the Light, I AM the Life, I AM the Love!

I AM THE WAY

"I AM the Way"[8]: this is also a complex saying, but let us delve into it.
Where does this way lead?—to the Kingdom of heaven. In one of the
confrontations with the Pharisees, Christ said to them, "You are from
below (*ek to kato*), but I am from above (*ek to ano*)."[9] These two "states"
were absolutely antithetical opposites, similar to the difference between
heaven and earth, or between body and spirit. And then, "Where I go

---

4   1 John 2:10
5   1 John 3:15
6   1 John 3:14, emphasis added.
7   John 14:6
8   John 14:6
9   John 8:23

you cannot follow, but will die in your sins, because you do not believe in Me." (The Jews asked whether He would kill Himself, because it was believed among them that he who kills himself is barred from Paradise; and if He was going to Hades, then they wouldn't follow Him there.) Christ also said to Nicodemus, "You must be born from above (*ek to ano*)."[10] Nicodemus asked if a man can enter his mother's womb again to be born a second time. He answered, "You won't be born again *of earth* to lead another earthly life, but you will be born *from above* that you may live a heavenly life."

Let's apply this to the Body and the Blood. When Christ offered to us His broken Body and Blood, He did not offer them as a theoretical blessing, but as a real, existential gift, to be incorporated into our actual nature. When the priest places the Body into your mouth, he is extremely careful to ensure that it has fully entered into your body, into your being; and after your partake of the Blood, the deacon offers you water to allow the gift to flow down completely into your entire body. Very close attention is given to every detail. "Take, eat of it all of you, for this is My body. Take, drink of it all of you, for this is My blood."[11] Christ's Body and Blood were given to fill us; then He ascended and entered into the Holy of Holies,[12] into the heavenlies, unto the Father. He thereby consecrated for us the *way*, a mystical, spiritual way, by His Body and Blood—for those who will believe. He who partakes of the Body and Blood immediately sets upon the Way.

Can we ever afterward be *ek to kato*? No, we are no longer from beneath. The proof is in Christ's prayer to the Father in John 17, when he says, "Those whom You gave me are not of this world, just as I am not of this world."[13] Also consider the wonderful saying of the Apostle Paul: "We have confidence to enter the Holiest by the Blood of Jesus,

10 John 3:7
11 Matt 26:26, 27
12 Heb 9:24
13 John 17:16

by a new and living way which He consecrated for us, through the veil, which is His body."[14] Ah, through the Body and Blood the way has been opened! *Ego eimi:* "I AM the Way." That teaching which He uttered so long ago we have eaten today! That teaching which was so difficult on men's ears, and was dismissed as a hard saying or just a bit of Greek philosophy, was manifested by the sacred mystery to be higher than every earthly philosophy.

I AM THE TRUTH

"I AM the Truth." Christ said to Pilate, "I have come to bear witness to the truth,"[15] and Pilate answered, "What is truth?" Pilate was a Roman; and although our governors today are not philosophers, it was necessary for any Roman chief or governor back then to have a philosophical education. Pilate was philosophically trained; hence his reply, "So what really is truth?" *Truth* was a perplexing topic among them; Plato and his kin could write many books about it without arriving at any satisfactory conclusion. Thus Christ could not have brought Pilate to understand "truth" in his frame of mind.

"My flesh is food in truth [indeed], and My blood is drink in truth [indeed]."[16] "In truth"—*alethea*. The translation doesn't actually reveal the full meaning. The effect of what He says is, "My Body is edible truth, and My Blood is drinkable truth." You see here how the Eucharist summarizes the loftiest and most difficult concepts and offers them to children! This mystery is transformed inside us into all of these different teachings. He who can comprehend such things, let him comprehend them; and he who cannot comprehend them, let him *believe* them. "My flesh is truth—*alethea*—that can be eaten."

---

14   Heb 10:19, 20
15   John 18:37
16   John 6:55. "In truth"—the literal sense of the Arabic.

What a strange thing! "And My Blood is truth that can be drunk." This edible and drinkable truth is founded on *faith*. If you believe, you will receive it; and if you receive it, you will arrive at all truth! This is what distinguishes Christianity from every other philosophy.

Consider the Brahmin philosophy of the Hindus. Go to the greatest Brahmin guru, a monk who has reached the highest spiritual levels of the Hindu philosophy and has sat over sixty years meditating alone on a mountain, and ask him this one question: "Have you arrived?"

He will bow his head between his knees and weep, and say, "I have not yet arrived."

Now go to any Christian who is truly sincere in the faith, and ask if he has arrived, and he will respond, "Alleluia! I have arrived."

What do we hear at the end of each liturgy but exclamations of "Praise Him . . . Alleluia!" over and over again?[17] What's the commotion all about? Why are the worshippers so happy? They have arrived. "I AM the Way and the Truth."

I AM THE LIVING BREAD THAT COMES DOWN FROM HEAVEN

"I AM the Living Bread that comes down from heaven."[18] This is an extremely hard concept for the mind to accept. He said, "Yes, and unless you eat of this bread, you cannot inherit eternal life."[19]

They replied, "Lord, give us this bread always." These were the five thousand fed by the five loaves and two fish who only wanted to be fed more.

When He got into the boat and departed, they followed after Him to the other shore of the lake, and He said, "Do you come to me

---

17 Ps 150 is sung at each Coptic liturgy during holy communion, with each line interrupted with an *Alleluia!*

18 John 6:51

19 John 6:53

again? You seek for the bread that perishes; seek rather for the bread of eternal life."[20]

When He said, "I AM the living bread that comes down from heaven," some stumbled, and even some of His disciples deserted and followed Him no more, complaining, "This is a hard saying. Who can accept it? How can He offer us His Body to eat?" But this is not a regular body, but a mystical, sacramental body.

When He offered His Body on Holy Thursday and said "take and eat," they looked and saw just bread; but they finally began to understand that these things were far above mere material notions. When you enter the altar today, for example, will you be given meat and bones? When you drink the cup, do you taste a thick, unpleasant liquid that cannot be swallowed? No, because the change is *mystical*. What was difficult to understand for those disciples who left Him was revealed and made clear on Holy Thursday as He said, "Take, eat, this is My body." *Ego eimi.* "I AM the Bread." The concept that was so difficult for the mind to grasp was made very, very easy when changed into terms of food and drink!

I AM WITH YOU UNTO THE END OF THE AGE

"I AM with you unto the end of the age."[21] He had said to them previously, "I will not leave you orphans.[22] I will be delivered to the Gentiles to be crucified; and on the third day, I will rise."[23] They experienced intense grief at these words and were very downcast. But His parting words after the Resurrection were a promise to be with them always, which included "I AM." (The promise was, "I AM with you unto the end of the age.") But how can that possibly be? *Here*, in

20 John 6:27
21 Matt 28:20
22 John 14:18
23 Luke 18:32

the mystery. When He offers us His Body and Blood, He offers them not as dead bodily members, but as living flesh and blood. These living flesh and blood together constitute a living sacrifice, a living personal entity, *ego eimi* Himself. We receive not a Body and Blood separate from Christ, but a living Body and Blood that are part of Him and He in them.

But please do not say to me, "Oh, I wish that my eyes were opened so that I could physically see Him in the sacrament but once!"

Do you really wish to see Him with your eyes? I will take you back 1,930 years and tell you, "Here He is physically; now are you satisfied?"

The Jews also saw Him physically, but they were offended at Him and sent Him to the Cross. Didn't even the disciples see and hear Him and witness so many wondrous things? Forgive me, but did they not even sit and eat with Him during the Last Supper? But since all this was taken in with the eyes of the mind and not with the eyes of faith, they also stumbled at the Cross and abandoned Him. So what good is it really to see Him physically? But we behold Him on the altar *mystically*.

I AM COMING QUICKLY

Finally, we have "I AM coming quickly," given to us by John the Evangelist in the Revelation.[24] So do we also eat "I AM coming quickly" in the Eucharist? Yes! You will remember that in the liturgy, the priest recites the words, "For every time you eat of this bread and drink of this cup, you proclaim My death, confess My resurrection, and remember Me till I come."[25] *Till I come*—this reference to the Second Coming is indeed an integral part of the Eucharist. When we partake

---

24 Rev 3:11
25 Institution Narrative of the Coptic Liturgy, prayed immediately before the Epiclesis, derived from 1 Cor 11:26.

of the Eucharist, we are partaking of the "wait" or "anticipation" of the Second Coming; and we wait not in anxiety but in faith.

We have thus concluded speaking about the first "mystery" in the Eucharist, which is *ego eimi*, the mystery of the transformation of "I AM" from a verbal expression to a liturgical sacrament. We now move to the second eucharistic "mystery," the divine Body of Christ.

THE DIVINE BODY OF CHRIST

I will ask one question to arouse your minds, that we might enter into the spiritual depths of this point. Christ, the Son of God, who is one with the Father and Holy Spirit, took a human body in order to save humanity, and humanity now abides in Christ. The true meaning of the Incarnation is that Christ "put on" all of humanity. This is the focal point of the hope of mankind. Without this single fact, the chasm between God and man would endure forever, and any movement across that chasm would be forever impossible. "You are from beneath, I am from above." So the first step God took in bringing man close to Him was the Incarnation of the Son; He took flesh and so forged a link between above and beneath.

Now here is the question: after Christ took human nature, after He was clothed in our flesh, could He at any time ever cast it off again? *Impossible*. For according to the faith of the Coptic Orthodox Church, the divine and human natures are united in a full and perfect union—without change, alteration, or confusion. The divine and human natures are joined in the person of our Lord Jesus Christ completely, eternally, and irreversibly. When our Lord ascended to heaven, with what did He ascend? He ascended with the flesh, meaning that He ascended with all of humanity.

When we say that He ascended with all humanity, we mean with those who have accepted the Cross, the Blood and the Body; and it is

Christ's eternal desire for all of humanity to become His Body. For outside His Body, humanity perishes without hope; but to enter into His Body is the one hope of mankind. And for this reason, God suffers very long with the entire world, and calls the entire world—hiddenly and openly, by action and by mystery, by sign and miracle, through the mind and through the heart, by the word of Scripture and by the miracle of life, by things expressible and inexpressible—He gathers mankind, from the East to the West, to become partakers in Christ. As the verse says, "Here am I and the children whom the LORD has given me!"[26] We are all those children.

Therefore, beloved, when we approach to eat the Body of Christ, each of us approaches as an individual; but after having eaten, no longer think of yourself as an individual person! You have become a member in the Body. Once I have partaken of the Eucharist, I am united to Him; and so no longer am I just "me." All of humanity is collected into a single person in Christ. Mankind itself began with a single person, and it will be completed in a single Person. Otherwise, the dispersing effects of sin and the Fall would be permanent. But Christ came to overcome such dispersion and separation; He came to gather the separate into one.[27]

This is why we consider Christ the second Adam. He is the *Head* of humanity, and we are the *Body*. So, as I asked before, could Christ ever cast off His Body? Impossible indeed! He is now in the presence of the Father with *us*; in truth, we have become His very Body, which He can never forsake. So I say, when we partake of the Body and Blood, we are being incorporated into that Body. As St. Paul says, "You are the members of His body,"[28] and in another astonishing statement, "We are members of His body, of His flesh and of His bones."[29]

26 Is 8:18 (NKJV)
27 Eph 2:14
28 1 Cor 12
29 Eph 5:30

What if, however, one severs himself from the Body? Farewell, then; he has no portion in Christ. You will find that once a Christian man feels his sinfulness, he hastens immediately to confession and cleansing. "How can I live for Christ this way?" he asks. "How can I take the member of Christ, myself, and make it the instrument of sin? Can one of Christ's members be decayed? Never!" That is why every Christian person, in any state of sin, should hasten quickly to be cleansed in the conscience, in the spirit, and mystically, for there is a sacrament of purification,[30] that he might be reinstated as a member of the Body.

I am a part in Christ: is He a part in me? No, He is *wholly* in me, for I am wholly united with Him. I as a *member*, but He as a *whole*, and we are all members of that one Body. Can I say, "What have I to do with my brother?" Can I be concerned only with saving my own skin? Can one hand say to the other, "You're worthless"? If so, then we wouldn't eat, for farming and harvest require two hands. That is why I said that I approach the mystery as an individual but am changed into one member among many.

If I approach the Eucharist by *myself*, that I may partake by *myself*, and save *myself*, and come out thinking, "What have I to do with these others?" such a state can never persist for long. The Eucharist can be received only on the truth that I am one among many members—a concept the Church calls "fellowship."[31] We fellowship collectively and equally in the one Body. This fellowship is founded on the idea that I have a stake in every other member, that what is mine is theirs, in Christ. But all of Christ is mine, and He is all yours too; so can one person then boast against another?

---

30 Confession or Penance.

31 The Arabic word *shareka* is stronger than the English *fellowship* in its connotations of co-participation or co-sharing in something great, best epitomized in the word *communion*, the full meaning being expressed in the Greek *oikonomia*.

Say I'm a metropolitan with a tall miter, and you're just a minor layman—according to the contrast drawn by St. James[32]—and we approach the Eucharist together; is there any inequality in the blessing we receive? Not a jot! There is no disparity between one Christian and another in the Lord! Actually, if you are greater in authority and responsibility, then the weaker member must receive greater honor than you;[33] and this will be only if our Christianity is genuine. But if our Christianity is spurious, then we will say to the bishop with the tall hat, "Stand here," and to the small layman we will say, "Go, take the back seat." But in Christ Jesus, there is neither rich nor poor, Greek nor Jew, slave nor free, male nor female.[34] All are one; and the communion of the Body and Blood is what produces the true union and equality in Christ. If you had received a greater proportion of Christ, then you could boast of being greater than I; but if you receive the same Christ that I do, then there is no difference between you and me or anyone in the Lord Jesus. This is the true meaning of fellowship in the Body, of comm-*union*,[35] the sharing of our joint oneness in Christ.

I want to explain for you a little how this oneness is accomplished "mystically," or—our language is so impoverished—"sacramentally." The Apostle Paul says, "The cup of blessing which we bless, is it not the communion of the Blood of Christ? The bread which we break, is it not the communion of the body of Christ?"[36] He is speaking to the believers in Corinth. "For we all partake of one bread."

Pay very close attention now. The one Body of Christ is offered mystically and sacramentally in *one bread*. Say I break a loaf of bread in pieces and say to several of you, "Take a piece," then one of you comes and tells me, "Give me the whole loaf." I'll reply, "The loaf has already

---

32 Jam 2:1–9
33 1 Cor 12:23
34 Gal 3:28
35 Abba Matta cites the English word to indicate the import of the suffix.
36 1 Cor 10:16

been divided and absorbed by the bodies of the brethren. I can't get it back for you."

Now let's move from this dead analogy to the living reality. If I break the living Body, the I AM's Body, during the liturgical fraction, and give it to several of the brethren, and say to each one, "Receive the whole," would that statement be correct? God knows it would be absolutely correct. Outwardly, it would appear that I divided the sacramental bread into pieces; but can I break Christ apart? Clearly not. On the material level I broke the bread (the mystical Body) into many little pieces, and the brethren ate them. But is the holy Body at that point, after having been consumed by everyone, really divided? It is not. It is still *one* Body and *one* bread—and the implications of this truth are enormous! The brethren who have partaken are now united. Each one might think he took a "piece" of the bread, but the fact is he took the whole Christ, who is indivisible. Whether they like it or not, they are now all one Body. And the same is true of the holy Blood.

This is the meaning of the second mystery of the Eucharist, the fellowship of the sacramental Body; yes, we are members of one Body. This ideal Christ attempted to realize during His three years of teaching, at the end of which He offered up that awesome prayer, saying, "I pray that they be one, as I am in You and You in me, that they be one in us."[37] But no mind can penetrate the depths of that request.

"How, O Lord, can humanity be made one in You? Each person goes his own way, has his own opinions, and believes his own theology and ideology." Ah, what humanity cannot achieve intellectually has been achieved ontologically![38] Each person might approach the Eucharist with his own particular ego and opinions and think himself independent of everyone else, but the Body and Blood cannot be received independently. Do you think you communicate on your own?

---

37 John 17:21
38 That is, in reality, or as a matter of fact.

Impossible. You are entering into the most profound and serious work of unification ever. And it unites you with every believer in all previous ages and generations.[39]

You are all weary now, and I cannot go into the third mystery of the Eucharist, the Mystery of the Kingdom. Let us pray together: "Our Lord Jesus Christ, who bestowed on us such great love, witnessed by all humanity from Adam till now; who knows the weakness of man, and what is in man, and the sin that prevents him from fellowship with the divinity; who offered Yourself this blessed day, as Body and Blood, to every human who accepts them, that whoever eats may have a portion in You, even though he be incapable of attaining to the full measure of faith in Christ—our Lord Jesus Christ, *reveal* Yourself to all mankind; for You are not just for Christians, but for every human being. Reveal Yourself, that the day of salvation might come quickly, that humanity might be one in love, that humanity might surmount its barriers, that humanity might arrive at true knowledge. Yes, Lord, grant every person through Your holy mystery to come to You in heaven, to Your Father, crying out, 'Abba, Father!' Bless Your Church, now and forever. Amen."

---

39   This is what Abba Matta says about the work of the Eucharist among
     different churches: "The eucharistic mystery unites the alpha and the
     omega, every nation and every race, every Catholic and Orthodox.
     Let them quarrel in Rome and in Alexandria all they want, but the
     Eucharist will unite them still. They are one in Christ, despite their
     theological differences. I heard lately that there's talk of 'reconciliation';
     well, let them reconcile all they want. Christ has already cast His net
     upon them; each group has already eaten the Eucharist. And even if the
     human will rejects union, and purposely sets up a thousand barriers to
     it, Christ has already made them one."

On the Resurrection

1979

Man bears in his body the marks of death since the day of his birth. The physicians corroborate this fact when they tell us that, from the moment a baby is born into the world and its body begins to interact with the external environment—especially when it contracts sickness and fevers—death begins to lay its first marks in the newborn body. Even when a person grows to full adulthood, every sickness that passes through the body leaves its mortal effects. I tell you, even the common cold can leave a dent in the body. If there were a device by which a man of fifty or sixty years could measure the amount of damage wrought in his body by disease, he could probably accurately predict the very day of his death. Yes, death is at work in us! And if our ears are open to the Word, and our morality is intact, our conscience will gradually realize that judgment is also at work in us.

In the potent words of St. Paul, the death of a righteous Man who committed no sin became justification for all men.[1] We have been justified, and we see in the Cross the annulment of two forces which had ruled the world and humanity since the Creation—death and judgment. It was a given that every person dies once, and then the judgment. But on the Cross, Christ's death conquered death; and by taking man's sin on Himself, He also conquered judgment. And thus the world and humanity have been loosed from the grip of those two tyrants, which had previously not allowed even the faintest slackening of the chains that bound us. How great is it that, through the Cross of Christ, we have been set free from death and judgment—and not by the Cross alone, but also by the Resurrection!

What words can be used to describe the Resurrection? Was it a "vision"? Can we refer to it as "the *vision* or *perception* of the Resurrection"? No; it is completely impossible that it was a mere vision. For when the disciples saw Christ risen from the dead, they didn't know Him; and even after He told them, "I AM," and allowed them to touch His Body, some still doubted.[2] So the Resurrection, beloved, is wholly outside the realm of visions.

Resurrection is rather a *new* phenomenon—a very different thing from birth and death alike. Those two events are the first and last things that demarcate the life of man; and we may ask if there can be anything outside the beginning and end of one's life? Yes, one thing—resurrection. Christ was insistent on pressing this point into the minds of the disciples. When He had descended from the Mount of Transfiguration, He charged them not to tell anyone of what had happened *until after the Resurrection*. They conferred together about what the resurrection from the dead meant, because nothing

---

1   See Rom 5:17.
2   Abba Matta seems to imply that, since everything in a "vision" is typically assumed to be true by the observer, the Resurrection must have been a real-life event, because many who saw the risen Lord were thrown into confusion and doubt.

of the like had ever happened before; how *could* the poor disciples understand? Even after our Lord rose from the dead, they still could not comprehend what had happened.

This is because the Resurrection far transcends the limits of the mind. You see, beloved, if the Resurrection is not subject to the laws of birth and death, then it is not subject to the laws of this physical life at all. And it is commonly known that this physical life is governed by two principles: *motion* and *time*. Motion, furthermore, assumes that a person is physically confined by certain dimensions. But resurrection submits to neither of these two; it is a *new dimension* of life. Christ entered the upper room while the doors were closed,[3] and He would appear to them in any place at any time—His physical life was no longer limited. So being previously absent from existence, resurrection is a new phenomenon that has entered our world, finally introduced to us by Christ. This is why we say that resurrection is neither birth nor death nor motion, but *another life*. The Bible calls it "eternal life" and also "a new creation."

But here we run into a dilemma. Since the resurrection is neither a vision, nor an idea to be controlled by logic, nor a phenomenon to be analyzed by the laws of this world, you will ask me how we can ever understand it. Well, this constitutes our "understanding" of the resurrection: *our new life*. I must now refer to those Bible scholars who have so wearied me, and who will weary you too, once God inflames your desire for Bible study and research. You will discover in them the most bitter criticism[4] of Scripture. And the criticism is bearable up until the point of our Lord's Passion, where it begins to cast severe doubts upon the narrative; and finally it comes to the Resurrection and denies it completely. This type of criticism has infiltrated most

3   John 20:19
4   Abba Matta uses the term in its technical sense of the (purportedly) scientific investigation into the origins, sources, and meanings of the Bible.

of the world's theological schools; and the majority of modern Bible interpreters do not even believe in the Resurrection. There are even bishops out there with theological degrees who do not believe!

I read recently of a Catholic bishop who stood up to preach on Easter day in a prominent church in Paris, where several thousands were in attendance. He proceeded to deny the Resurrection, telling them that there isn't sufficient reason to believe, but that it is possible to believe in Christ apart from the Resurrection.

There was a young Russian priest present—and you know those Russians who, despite the calamity[5] that descended upon their heads, were preserved by God like the remnant of prophets in the Old Testament.[6] This Russian priest stood up and raised his hand—though in the West such an action is prohibited in church, especially before a bishop—and said, "May I say something?"

The bishop hesitated but permitted the priest to speak. He walked up before the congregation and cried out at the top of his lungs, "Christ is risen!"

And the people cried back, "Truly He is risen!"

The priest sat back down, but the bishop could not continue his sermon.

"Christ is risen" and "Truly He is risen" have been planted in our bones! Scholars may reject it, and expunge it from their theology, and demean it in their science, and strangle those poor, simple disciples in their ravaging grip, but to no avail—the Resurrection is planted in our flesh, in our blood and our bones. I want to say again that resurrection is not mere vision, contemplation, theory, or logic: it is *life*. And he who does not receive it as life will end up like that bishop and like those scholars. Resurrection, beloved, is the action of a new life in man. It

---

5   Communism and the persecution of the Soviet era.
6   Is 1:9

is the new creation. "You must be born of water and Spirit"[7]—born, that is, of earth beneath and of heaven above. "You must be born from above."[8] Here's a seeming difficulty, for who can take me up to heaven to be reborn? Christ made the act possible for us by causing heaven to send down its grace to us through the mystery.[9]

Let us go deeper into our discussion. The key to our discourse about resurrection this evening will be found in Matthew 27. "Christ cried out with a loud voice and gave up the spirit. And the temple's veil was torn in two from top to bottom."[10] This was the beginning of the Resurrection's activity! The veil separated the holy place from the holy of holies; and the rending of the veil was an emblem of the dissolution of the barrier that separated us from God.[11] "The earth quaked and the rocks were split." Note that these words clearly point to a prior comment in Scripture—who spoke these words before? Or when will that earthquake and that rending of the rocks occur? It was Christ Himself who designated these as the signs of the general resurrection, which will occur when He comes in His glory.[12]

Note well here that His Resurrection is being indicated as the dawn of the general resurrection. This connection is our topic for the evening: Christ's Resurrection and our resurrection. I told you before that the Resurrection has meaning for our lives and is now at work in us. As we speak, we must recognize that work, or else the Resurrection will be meaningless to us. How often has this happened, and how commonly do we say, "Christ is risen," as if it were just an event in the remote past far removed from us! And so our lives follow the same sad routine, day in and day out, as if there were no Christ at all.

---

7   John 3:5
8   John 3:3. An alternate translation to "born again."
9   Baptism, John 3.
10 Matt 27:51
11 See Heb 9.
12 Matt 24:7

"The graves were opened; and many bodies of the saints who had fallen asleep were raised; and coming out of their graves after His resurrection, they went into the holy city and appeared to many."[13] What lofty and wonderful mystery! What an extraordinary link has the Gospel revealed between the Resurrection of Christ and the resurrection of man! The graves were opened, and the bodies of the dead appeared but remained motionless; and as the Gospel tells us, they emerged from the graves after His Resurrection. These are mysteries that transcend time and space, as well as the limits of our understanding. Once Christ died on the Cross, the graves were opened, which is a clear sign to us that Christ's death is directly linked to the graves of men.

How great art thou, O Church! The hymn that we will say throughout the entire holy fifty days[14] declares, "By death He trampled upon death. And to those in the grave He granted eternal life." This hymn, the oldest ecclesiastical rite relating to the Resurrection, was inherited directly from St. Matthew! And note its direct relation to Christ's death on the Cross. Of course, you might have protested secretly during our discussion of the Resurrection and said to yourself, "Why can't we stick to the topic? Why is he bringing us back to Good Friday and the Cross?" But I will answer, review your Church's rites.

They entered the holy city and appeared to many—this is a very important point. The appearance of these risen saints—which included Jeremiah, Isaiah, and the prophets—was known to the Jews according to their tradition passed down from *hakeem*[15] to *hakeem*. Now, when a resurrection would occur, a type of revelation would happen that gave an observer the ability to recognize the risen individual. Those "many" received the ability to see and became witnesses, and so laid down

13 Matt 27:52, 53
14 The Orthodox Church observes a fifty-day celebratory period for the Resurrection following Easter Sunday.
15 A Jewish wise man.

the foundation for the Church's tradition and theology. Where else do we get our hymnology? The Church never invents her theology. No, the theology of the Coptic Orthodox Church—indeed the nature of theology in general—is not speculative but rather *inherited*. So the phrase "He trampled death by death" is not a mere lyrical invention, but a theological truth witnessed to by those who rose from their graves. And Peter speaks the truth when he says that He descended into Hades[16] (words we have incorporated into the liturgy), for how would they have risen from the grave unless their souls were first set loose? Their souls were freed in Hades, and they awaited the Resurrection of the Lord to appear in the city. So along with the announcement of the angels, the women, and the disciples regarding the Resurrection, there was the additional witness of these saints who appeared to many.

I have been saying that the Lord's death exerted a living, active influence upon the dead. We must also gain advantage from this influence ourselves! For the Lord's death works good in us too. It abolished the authority of death which separated man from God, and it tore the veil from top to bottom and paved the way to the Resurrection. The Resurrection then freed the dead from the bonds of time and space. Human flesh is "bound" in the grave; that is, even though dissolved to dust, the body is controlled by the dictates and changeableness of matter. But now even matter is overcome, for the Resurrection conquered the laws of matter. The ultimate attribute of matter is that it changes and perishes; I am not supposed to say that matter can be "destroyed." But modern science has split the atom, and split its protons and electrons, and ended up with a basic "dust" that is only a series of numbers on paper; and thus matter has been reduced to nothingness. The resurrection is not subject to such "matter." Remember how Paul, when confronted with the question of what the resurrection body will be like, returns the stern reply, "Foolish one! You

---

16   1 Pet 3:19

sow a seed but it sprouts a different body."[17] Such is the resurrection—
how beautifully Paul describes it!—independent of the appearances
and whims of matter. And since it is superior to the laws of matter,
how easily can it gather a heap of dust—even if blown out over all the
oceans—to reconstitute the body as it was!

The appearance of the departed saints in the city was, to repeat,
the dawn of the coming general resurrection. Let us thank God then
that the resurrection is not a future event that we wearily wait for but
has already begun on earth! Yes, the new creation has begun! How
else are we baptized? How else do we receive the Holy Spirit? The
dawn of salvation has entered the world, and the light of that dawn
has reached our eyes through baptism. So those who rose that day are
not waiting for us to join them, but we have joined in that resurrection
already, through baptism.[18] We have risen from the grave, and death is
no more a barrier to eternal life! Quite the reverse: death has become a
door to eternal life. Or rather, death is the torn veil through which we
can enter into the Holy of Holies. And isn't the torn veil His broken
Body? Doesn't this remind us of the broken Body and shed Blood on
the Cross? Doesn't all this point to the Eucharist? Isn't this all granted
through baptism? What amazing correlations!

You might be saying now, "If only I could have been there to see
those great saints of the Old Testament who entered the holy city!"
But better still, we are *partakers* with them! That dawn of salvation
that broke upon the earth on the day of Christ's Resurrection became,
in fact, the inheritance of *all* humanity. All thanks and praise be to
Christ! We have been made fellow heirs with the saints! Didn't Paul
call us members of the household of God?[19] We who were afar off
and aliens from the sheepfold of Israel—without God or hope in this

---

17 1 Cor 15:35–37
18 Rom 6:3–5
19 Eph 2:19

world—have been brought near by the Blood of Christ, and the two have been made into one Body, a new man in Christ Jesus![20] We have received this by our acceptance of that baptism from heaven, which is by water and the Spirit. We have been buried and raised with Christ, and so our mortal graves have been rent and opened. The fatality of our sin has been stripped; we have received the light of the Resurrection and have entered that dawn of salvation upon which the night will never fall in our hearts!

Have you perceived the power of resurrection yet? Have you felt its movements within you? We are not just meditating on the Resurrection now, but actually are partaking in it! We *live* by it. We *exist* in it. We are *enlightened* by it. The Light has already entered, brethren: "I am the light of the world."[21] And we are also the light of the world[22]—meaning partakers of resurrection.

Remember the wonderful saying, "And so we have the prophetic word confirmed, which you do well to heed as a light that shines in a dark place, until the day dawns and the morning star rises in your hearts."[23] Just as a blind man tries to feel his way along a wall, so must we be continually attempting to grasp the deep meanings of the Bible. We must compare prophecy to prophecy, to commentary, to quotation, and so on, until we begin to perceive the first few shreds of light. And the "morning star" was made plain by John in the Apocalypse: "I am the bright and morning star."[24] I pray that this star and that dawn be not neglected by us, Abbas! I pray that baptism be not a dead ritual, and the Resurrection of Christ a mere topic of biblical research!

The dawn has come and will never fade from the hearts of the saints. Every person who is buried and risen with Christ is a saint!

---

20   Eph 2:12, 13
21   John 8:12
22   Matt 5:14
23   2 Pet 1:19
24   Rev 22:15

Every believer is a member of the holy Body[25]—and this is the origin of our sainthood. "I write to the *saints* who are in Ephesus."[26] One day we will see Him as He is; the light of His countenance will be reflected on our faces, and we will be like Him.

---

25 1 Cor 12:12
26 Eph 1:1

More Books from
Ancient Faith Publishing

THE SCENT OF HOLINESS

by Constantina R. Palmer
Every monastery exudes the scent of holiness, but women's monasteries have their own special flavor. Join Constantina Palmer as she makes frequent pilgrimages to a women's monastery in Greece and absorbs the nuns' particular approach to their spiritual life. If you're a woman who's read of Mount Athos and longed to partake of its grace-filled atmosphere, this book is for you. Men who wish to understand how women's spirituality differs from their own will find it a fascinating read as well. ISBN: 978-1-936270-42-2

TRAVELING COMPANIONS

by Christopher Moorey
Do you long to establish a relationship with the saints, but find them— or the volumes written about them—a little intimidating? The saints started out as ordinary Christians, just like us, and they are waiting

to accompany us on our journey to heaven if we will only reach out our hands. *Traveling Companions* is a manageable volume that briefly introduces saints from a variety of times, places, and walks of life, all in language that brings them close to contemporary readers' lives. You're sure to find companions here that you will be happy to walk with all the way to the Kingdom. ISBN: 978-1-936270-47-7

THE CHRISTIAN OLD TESTAMENT

by Lawrence R. Farley
Many Christians see the Old Testament as "the other Testament": a source of exciting stories to tell the kids, but not very relevant to the Christian life. The Christian Old Testament reveals the Hebrew Scriptures as the essential context of Christianity, as well as a many-layered revelation of Christ Himself. Follow along as Fr. Lawrence Farley explores the Christian significance of every book of the Old Testament. ISBN: 978-1-936270-53-8

BREAD & WATER, WINE & OIL

by Archimandrite Meletios Webber
According to two thousand years of experience, Orthodoxy shows us how to be transformed by the renewing of our mind—a process that is aided by participation in the traditional ascetic practices and Mysteries of the Church. In this unique and accessible book, Archimandrite Meletios Webber first explores the role of mystery in the Christian life, then walks the reader through the seven major Mysteries of the Orthodox Church, showing the way to a richer, fuller life in Christ. ISBN: 978-1-888212-91-4

All books available at store.ancientfaith.com
Explore great Orthodox audio content at www.ancientfaith.com